SEVILLE TRAVEL GUIDE 2025

Discover Andalusia's Heart – History, Flamenco, Tapas, and Hidden Gems"

Van J. Pulliam

SEVILLE, SPAIN

View larger map

Alfonsito
BRUNCH CAFE

Restaurant
Milonga's |
Argentinian

Seville

C. Juan de Vera

C. Luis Montoto

C. Vidrio

C. Timtes

C. Alberto Durero

Plaza de los
Zurradores

Pizzeria Carlos Sevilla
Pizza

Abantal
Fine Dining

Caños de Carm

Mutua Cesma

Baja Bikes

Google

Keyboard shortcuts   Map data ©2025 Google, Inst. Geogr. Nacional   Terms   Report a map error

SCAN THE QR CODE

1. Open your phone's camera – Most modern smartphones have a built-in QR scanner in the camera app.
2. Point the camera at the QR code – Make sure the code is fully visible on your screen.
3. Wait for a notification – A link should appear on your screen.
4. Tap the link – This will take you to the website or content linked to the QR code.

TABLE OF CONTENTS

INTRODUCTION

There is a rhythm to Seville, a heartbeat that pulses through its cobbled streets, sun-drenched plazas, and Moorish courtyards. It is the rhythm of flamenco's fiery passion, the steady clip-clop of horses pulling carriages past centuries-old buildings, and the murmur of laughter spilling out of tapas bars as locals sip on chilled sherry. This city is a tapestry of history and culture, where the past and present weave together seamlessly to create an experience unlike any other. Whether you are drawn by its architectural splendor, its rich culinary traditions, or the warmth of its people, Seville is not just a place to visit—it is a place to feel, to taste, and to fall in love with.

There is a reason why Seville remains one of the most enchanting destinations in Spain. It is a city that has been shaped by empires, from the Romans who first recognized its strategic importance to the Moors who left behind an architectural legacy that still dazzles visitors today. It is the birthplace of flamenco, a city that celebrates life with festivals so grand that they redefine the meaning of joy. Here, history is not confined to museum walls—it is alive in the orange-scented air of Barrio Santa Cruz, in the towering majesty of the Giralda, and in the whisper of centuries-old prayers inside the grand Seville Cathedral.

If ever there was a perfect time to visit Seville, it is now. The city has always been a destination that beckons travelers, but in 2025, it shines even brighter. Recent restorations of key monuments have revealed architectural details long hidden from view, making iconic sights like the Alcázar and Plaza de España even more breathtaking. Culinary trends are transforming traditional tapas culture, blending the old with the new in a way that excites even the most seasoned food lovers. Sustainability initiatives are making it easier to explore the city responsibly, allowing visitors to experience its wonders while preserving its beauty for generations to come.

Beyond its timeless appeal, Seville in 2025 offers a dynamic mix of modernity and tradition. This year, new cultural events and exhibitions celebrate Andalusian heritage with fresh perspectives, while innovative urban projects enhance the city's walkability, making it more inviting than ever for travelers who want to lose themselves in its winding streets. Whether you're a first-time visitor or someone returning to deepen your love affair with Seville, this year promises an experience that is both authentic and exhilarating.

Seville is not a city that merely exists—it performs. It seduces. It tells stories with every carved archway, every hidden courtyard, every haunting note of a flamenco song. It is a city that invites you to slow down, to savor the details, to truly immerse yourself in its way of life. The essence of

Seville is best captured in its flamenco tablaos, where the raw emotion of the dance transports audiences to another world. It is felt in the Feria de Abril, when the city transforms into a spectacle of color, music, and dance, reminding visitors that joy is meant to be celebrated in grand fashion. It is seen in the meticulous beauty of its Mudéjar palaces and baroque churches, where every tile and fresco whispers a piece of history.

But Seville is not just about its famous landmarks—it is also about the quiet moments. A morning café con leche in a hidden plaza, where time seems to stand still. A late-night stroll along the Guadalquivir River, as the golden lights of the Torre del Oro shimmer on the water. A chance conversation with a local, who tells you about a tiny, family-run tapas bar where the best jamón ibérico in town is served. It is in these moments that Seville becomes more than a destination. It becomes a feeling.

This book is not just a travel guide—it is your companion to Seville, a carefully crafted roadmap that will help you uncover both the celebrated highlights and the hidden treasures of this remarkable city. It is designed to inspire, to inform, and to make your journey effortless. Each chapter delves into a different aspect of Seville, from its historic neighborhoods and iconic sights to its rich traditions, cuisine, and day-trip possibilities. You'll find practical tips on everything from navigating public transport to selecting the best places to stay, along with insider recommendations that will take your experience beyond the usual tourist trails. Whether you prefer a meticulously planned itinerary or the thrill of spontaneous exploration, this guide will equip you with everything you need to make the most of your time in Seville.

By the time you reach the last page of this book, my hope is that Seville will no longer be just a destination on your map—it will be a part of you. Because Seville is not just a place to see. It is a city to be felt, to be lived, to be remembered long after you have left. So, let's begin your journey. Seville is waiting for you.

Why Seville in 2025?

Seville has always been a city that captivates the senses, but in 2025, it shines even brighter. There is a renewed energy in its streets, a perfect blend of tradition and modernity that makes this the ideal time to visit. The city has undergone thoughtful restorations, revealing hidden details in its architectural masterpieces, making landmarks like the Alcázar, the Cathedral, and Plaza de España more breathtaking than ever. Cultural events are evolving, offering fresh perspectives on Andalusian heritage while maintaining the soul of Seville's traditions. The culinary scene is thriving, as chefs reinterpret classic tapas with innovative twists, and new rooftop bars provide some of the best sunset views over the city's historic skyline.

Sustainability initiatives are changing the way travelers experience Seville, with pedestrian-friendly projects making it easier to wander through its enchanting streets, improved public transport options, and a growing emphasis on eco-friendly tourism. The Guadalquivir River, once a bustling trade route, is now seeing new life with riverfront developments and scenic walks that bring a fresh perspective to the city's timeless beauty. Festivals like Feria de Abril and Semana Santa continue to be grand spectacles, but with enhanced accessibility and cultural experiences that allow visitors to engage with them on a deeper level.

Beyond the city itself, 2025 brings exciting opportunities for day trips to nearby destinations like Córdoba, Jerez, and Doñana National Park, where nature, history, and gastronomy come together to offer unforgettable adventures. Whether you are visiting Seville for the first time or returning to rediscover its magic, this year promises an experience that is both authentic and exhilarating. Seville in 2025 is a city that invites you to immerse yourself completely, to lose track of time in its hidden plazas, to feel the passion of its music and dance, to indulge in its rich flavors, and to witness a place where history is not just remembered but lived.

A City of Passion, History, and Flamenco

Seville is not just a city; it is an experience that unfolds in layers, each one richer than the last. It is a place where history is not confined to textbooks but is alive in the very stones of its streets, where passion is not just an emotion but a way of life, and where flamenco is not merely a performance but the beating heart of the city's soul. From the moment you arrive, Seville surrounds you with an energy that is impossible to ignore. The scent of orange blossoms drifts through the air, the golden light bathes the city in a warm glow, and the sound of a flamenco guitar echoes down an alleyway, carrying with it centuries of longing, love, and defiance.

Few places in the world embody passion as completely as Seville does. It is in the way people speak, animated and expressive, their words punctuated with laughter and gestures. It is in the way they live, embracing the joy of a long lunch, the excitement of a festival, or the simple pleasure of an evening paseo through the streets. Nowhere is this passion more evident than in flamenco, the soul-stirring art form that was born in the heart of Andalusia. To witness flamenco in Seville is to see raw emotion transformed into movement and sound, the dancer's feet striking the floor in perfect rhythm with the mournful wail of the cantaor, the guitarist weaving a melody that seems to pull at something deep within. It is more than music; it is storytelling at its most primal and powerful.

But Seville is also a city that wears its history proudly. Once a major port of the Spanish Empire, it was here that explorers like Christopher Columbus set sail into the unknown, and here that the riches of the New World poured into Spain, shaping the city into one of Europe's grandest. The legacy of its Moorish past is written in the delicate arches of the Alcázar, where intricate tilework and lush gardens transport visitors to another time. The grandeur of its Catholic heritage is evident in the awe-inspiring Seville Cathedral, a masterpiece that stands as a symbol of the city's power and devotion. The Jewish quarter of Santa Cruz tells another story, one of narrow winding streets, hidden courtyards, and whispers of a time when cultures mingled and thrived together.

Seville is a city of contrasts—of fiery celebrations and quiet siestas, of ancient traditions and modern reinventions, of intense passion and laid-back charm. It is a place where every corner holds a story, every building a piece of history, and every moment the potential to be unforgettable. To visit Seville is to step into a living work of art, where the past and present dance together in perfect harmony, and where, if you listen closely, you can hear the heartbeat of the city in the rhythm of flamenco.

How to Use This Guide

This book is more than just a collection of recommendations—it is your personal gateway to experiencing Seville in a way that feels effortless, immersive, and deeply rewarding. Whether you are here for a short visit or a long stay, whether you prefer to plan every detail or let the city surprise you, this guide is designed to be your companion, offering insights that go beyond the obvious and leading you toward both the celebrated highlights and the hidden treasures of Seville.

Rather than overwhelming you with rigid itineraries, this book unfolds naturally, just as your experience in Seville should. You will be guided through the city's most iconic sights—the breathtaking Alcázar, the majestic Seville Cathedral, the vibrant Plaza de España—while also discovering tucked-away plazas, atmospheric tapas bars, and local secrets that make the city so irresistible. It will introduce you to Seville's rich history, unraveling its layers of Moorish, Jewish, and Catholic influences, all while weaving in the modern pulse of a city that continues to evolve. Along the way, you will find practical tips on everything from navigating public transport to understanding local customs, ensuring that your time here is as smooth as it is unforgettable.

This guide does not expect you to rush from place to place, checking sights off a list. Instead, it encourages you to slow down, to savor the rhythm of the city, to lose yourself in its streets and let serendipity lead the way. It will help you know when to join the locals in their long afternoon meals, when to seek out the quiet beauty of a courtyard garden, and when to step into the night to experience the raw energy of flamenco. You will find recommendations on where to eat, where to stay, and where to catch the most stunning sunset views, but more importantly, you will gain a sense of how to truly connect with Seville, to experience it not as an outsider, but as someone who understands its heart.

By the time you finish this book, my hope is that Seville will feel familiar, as if you have always known it. More than just a destination, it will become a place that lingers in your memory, calling you back long after you have left. However you choose to explore, let this guide be your starting point, your inspiration, and your key to unlocking all the beauty, history, and magic that Seville has to offer.

CHAPTER 1: GETTING TO SEVILLE

Arriving by Air, Train, and Road

Arriving in Seville is the beginning of an unforgettable journey, and whether you come by air, train, or road, the city welcomes you with ease and efficiency. If you are flying in, Seville's San Pablo Airport (SVQ) is your gateway, located just a short drive from the city center. Well-connected to major European hubs, it offers both international and domestic flights, making it a convenient entry point for travelers from all over the world. Upon landing, you can reach the heart of Seville by taxi, airport shuttle, or even a rental car if you plan to explore the wider Andalusian region. The airport bus service, known as the EA (Especial Aeropuerto), provides a reliable and affordable option, running regularly between the terminal and key locations in the city, including Santa Justa train station and the historic center.

For those arriving by train, Santa Justa station serves as Seville's main railway hub, linking the city to the rest of Spain with speed and comfort. The high-speed AVE trains make travel from Madrid effortless, with a journey time of just two and a half hours, while regional and long-distance trains connect Seville to other major destinations like Barcelona, Valencia, and Málaga. Stepping off the train, you will find yourself just minutes from the heart of the city, with taxis, buses, and even electric scooters readily available to take you wherever you need to go. Train travel in Spain is not just about convenience; it is an experience in itself, offering scenic views of the Andalusian countryside and the chance to travel in comfort without the hassle of airport security lines.

If you prefer the freedom of the open road, arriving in Seville by car can be a scenic and flexible way to explore the region. The city is well connected by Spain's excellent highway network, with major routes like the A-4 linking Seville to Madrid, the A-92 stretching across Andalusia, and the AP-4 providing a direct route from Cádiz. Driving into Seville, however, requires some planning, as the historic center is a maze of narrow, winding streets, many of which are pedestrian-only or restricted to local traffic. If you are staying in the city, parking in one of the designated public garages is often the best option, allowing you to explore on foot without the stress of navigating the tight alleyways. For those embarking on a road trip through southern Spain, Seville is a perfect starting point, offering easy access to nearby gems like Córdoba, Ronda, and the sun-soaked beaches of the Costa de la Luz.

However you choose to arrive, Seville embraces visitors with open arms, setting the stage for an experience that is as smooth as it is unforgettable. Whether you step off a plane, glide in on a high-speed train, or roll into town by car, the moment you arrive, you will feel the magic of Seville waiting to unfold.

Best Times to Visit in 2025

Seville is a city that dazzles year-round, but choosing the best time to visit in 2025 depends on what kind of experience you seek. Each season brings its own magic, shaping the city's rhythm, atmosphere, and even the way locals go about their daily lives. From grand festivals to peaceful, sun-soaked afternoons, timing your visit well can make all the difference in how you connect with Seville's vibrant soul.

Spring is arguably the most enchanting time to visit, when Seville bursts into full bloom, and the city's two most iconic festivals—Semana Santa and Feria de Abril—transform the streets into a spectacle of tradition, passion, and celebration. March and April offer near-perfect weather, with warm days, cool evenings, and the scent of orange blossoms filling the air. Semana Santa, the city's famed Holy Week, is a deeply moving experience, as solemn processions wind through the streets with candlelit floats and hauntingly beautiful music. Just weeks later, the Feria de Abril offers a completely different kind of energy—a week-long party of flamenco, horse parades, and joyful gatherings in colorful casetas. If you want to see Seville at its most festive, spring is the time to come, but it is also when the city is at its busiest, so booking accommodations early is essential.

As summer approaches, Seville's temperatures soar, with daytime highs regularly exceeding 40°C (104°F). While this can be challenging for those unaccustomed to the heat, summer has its own charm, especially in the evenings when life shifts outdoors. Rooftop terraces, late-night flamenco shows, and lively riverfront bars create an electric atmosphere, while day trips to nearby coastal towns provide a welcome escape to the sea. If you visit in summer, adjusting to the local rhythm—long siestas, late dinners, and exploring in the cooler morning and evening hours—will make all the difference.

Autumn brings a golden warmth to the city, with September and October offering a more relaxed alternative to the intensity of spring. The summer crowds have faded, yet the weather remains pleasant, making it the perfect time for sightseeing, leisurely strolls through the Alcázar's gardens, and enjoying tapas on outdoor terraces. Cultural events continue to thrive, with film festivals, art exhibitions, and smaller local fairs adding to the season's appeal. This is a time when Seville reveals a quieter, more introspective side—ideal for those who want to experience its beauty without the overwhelming festival crowds.

Winter, though often overlooked, can be a wonderful time to visit. The holiday season brings a special charm, with Christmas markets, dazzling light displays, and the lively celebrations of Día de los Reyes Magos (Three Kings' Day) in early January. The cooler temperatures make exploring the city much more comfortable, and with fewer tourists, you can enjoy Seville's major landmarks with a sense of calm and intimacy. It is also a great time to experience the local food scene, as cozy tapas bars become the perfect refuge for indulging in warm, comforting Andalusian dishes.

In 2025, Seville promises a year filled with cultural highlights, new exhibitions, and the timeless traditions that make it one of Spain's most captivating cities. Whether you come for the grandeur of spring, the sultry nights of summer, the golden beauty of autumn, or the quiet charm of winter, there is never a wrong time to visit—only the time that speaks to the kind of journey you seek. Seville will be waiting, ready to welcome you in its own unforgettable way.

Visa and Entry Requirements

Traveling to Seville in 2025 is an exciting prospect, and ensuring a smooth arrival begins with understanding Spain's visa and entry requirements. As part of the Schengen Zone, Spain follows standard European entry rules, meaning your specific requirements will depend on your nationality, the length of your stay, and the purpose of your visit.

For citizens of the European Union, Schengen Area countries, and several visa-exempt nations—including the United States, Canada, the United Kingdom, Australia, and Japan—entry into Spain for tourism or business purposes is straightforward. Visitors from these countries can stay for up to 90 days within a 180-day period without a visa. However, as of 2025, travelers from visa-exempt countries will be required to obtain an ETIAS (European Travel Information and Authorization System) approval before their trip. This is a quick online authorization process, similar to the U.S. ESTA system, and should be completed in advance to avoid any last-minute travel disruptions.

For those who require a visa, a Schengen visa must be obtained from the Spanish consulate or embassy in your home country before departure. This visa generally allows travel within all Schengen countries for up to 90 days. The application typically requires proof of accommodation, travel insurance covering at least €30,000 in medical expenses, proof of sufficient funds, and a return ticket or onward travel plans.

If you plan to stay longer, whether for work, study, or extended travel, you will need to apply for the appropriate visa or residence permit before arriving in Spain. Digital nomads and remote workers may also find opportunities through Spain's digital nomad visa, which allows non-EU citizens to live and work remotely from Spain for an extended period.

Upon arrival in Spain, passport control may require proof of accommodation, a return ticket, and evidence of sufficient funds for your stay. If you are traveling between Schengen countries, border checks are usually minimal, but it is always advisable to carry identification.

While entry into Spain is generally hassle-free for most travelers, it is always best to check the latest requirements before your trip, as regulations can change. With the right preparation, you can focus on what really matters— immersing yourself in the beauty, history, and excitement of Seville.

CHAPTER 2: EXPLORING THE HEART OF SEVILLE

The Historic Center: A Walk Through Time

Seville's historic center is not just the heart of the city; it is a journey through centuries of history, where every street, square, and building tells a story. Walking through its labyrinthine alleys and grand plazas feels like stepping into a living museum, where Moorish, Gothic, Renaissance, and Baroque influences intertwine seamlessly. It is a place where time slows, where echoes of the past linger in the air, and where every turn reveals something extraordinary—an ornate church façade, a hidden courtyard overflowing with bougainvillea, or the distant strumming of a flamenco guitar drifting from an open window.

At the center of it all stands the awe-inspiring Seville Cathedral, a structure so grand it dominates the skyline. Built on the site of a former mosque, it remains one of the largest Gothic cathedrals in the world, housing treasures that range from the golden splendor of the Main Altar to the tomb of Christopher Columbus. Rising beside it is La Giralda, the iconic bell tower that was once a minaret, its Moorish origins still visible despite the later additions. Climbing to the top rewards visitors with breathtaking panoramic views, a reminder of how Seville's history unfolds in layers, one era built upon the foundations of another.

Just steps away lies the Real Alcázar, a palace so enchanting it defies time itself. Originally a Moorish fortress, it evolved into a masterpiece of Mudejar architecture, with intricate tilework, horseshoe arches, and lush gardens that feel like a sanctuary in the middle of the city. Wandering through its courtyards, it is easy to imagine the echoes of sultans, kings, and queens who once called this place home. Even today, the Spanish royal family still uses parts of the palace, making it the oldest royal residence in Europe still in use.

From there, the historic quarter unfolds in a maze of narrow streets that lead into the enchanting Barrio de Santa Cruz, the former Jewish quarter. This is where Seville feels most intimate, with whitewashed houses, flower-filled balconies, and small plazas shaded by orange trees. The air is thick with history, yet the atmosphere is warm and inviting, as if the city itself is welcoming you to slow down and savor the moment. It is here, in the small tapas bars tucked away in quiet corners, that the spirit of Seville comes alive—where locals gather to sip fino sherry and share plates of jamón ibérico, where laughter spills into the streets, and where time seems to stand still.

Beyond Santa Cruz, the grand Plaza de España offers a striking contrast, an architectural marvel built for the Ibero-American Exposition of 1929. With its sweeping semi-circular design, elaborate bridges, and colorful ceramic tiles depicting Spain's provinces, it is a symbol of the city's ambition and artistic grandeur. Though a relatively recent addition to Seville's historic landscape, it feels like an integral part of its soul, a place where the past and present meet in a stunning display of beauty and craftsmanship.

Exploring Seville's historic center is not about following a strict itinerary; it is about wandering, getting lost, and allowing the city to reveal itself to you piece by piece. It is about stepping into the past while feeling the vibrant pulse of the present. It is about the quiet awe of standing before centuries-old wonders and the joy of stumbling upon something unexpected—a hidden courtyard, a lively street performer, or a centuries-old shop selling handmade ceramics. In Seville, history is not just something to be admired; it is something to be felt, experienced, and lived.

Barrio Santa Cruz: The Old Jewish Quarter

Barrio Santa Cruz is more than just one of Seville's most picturesque neighborhoods—it is the very essence of the city's layered history, where Moorish, Jewish, and Christian influences intertwine in a maze of narrow alleys, sun-dappled plazas, and whitewashed houses adorned with cascading flowers. Tucked within the heart of the historic center, this quarter was once the Jewish district of medieval Seville, a place of both prosperity and tragedy, where centuries of cultural richness were overshadowed by the forced expulsion of Spain's Jewish population in 1492. Today, however, Santa Cruz lives on as a neighborhood that breathes history at every corner, drawing visitors into its quiet courtyards, hidden patios, and intimate, winding streets that seem designed for getting delightfully lost.

Walking through Santa Cruz is like stepping back in time, where the streets were deliberately built to be narrow not only for defense but also to offer shade from the intense Andalusian sun. The effect is enchanting, as twisting passageways open unexpectedly into tranquil plazas, where orange trees cast dappled shadows and the sound of trickling fountains provides a peaceful soundtrack to the neighborhood's charm. Plaza de Santa Cruz, once the site of a Jewish synagogue, now holds a small but elegant garden with a central iron cross, a quiet nod to the area's layered past. Nearby, Plaza de Doña Elvira is one of the most romantic spots in the city, its benches lined with intricate azulejo tiles and its small restaurants spilling out onto the square, inviting visitors to linger over a glass of wine and a plate of tapas.

Despite its beauty, Santa Cruz holds echoes of its painful history. Before the 15th century, Seville's Jewish community thrived here, contributing to the city's cultural and intellectual life. But in the late 1300s, anti-Jewish riots swept through Spain, and by 1492, the Alhambra Decree issued by Ferdinand and Isabella forced all Jews to convert to Christianity or leave Spain entirely. What was once a flourishing neighborhood became a ghost of itself, yet traces of its past remain—not in grand monuments, but in the quiet corners, the hidden courtyards, and the stories whispered through the centuries. Calle de la Susona is one such place, a narrow street named after Susona, a Jewish woman who, according to legend, betrayed her own community to protect her Christian lover, only to suffer a tragic fate herself. Her story lingers in the street that bears her name, a haunting reminder of the neighborhood's layered past.

Beyond its historical weight, Santa Cruz today is a place of vibrant life, where past and present coexist in perfect harmony. The scent of jasmine drifts through the air as locals and visitors alike meander past charming boutiques selling hand-painted ceramics, delicate lace fans, and intricate silverwork. At night, the quarter takes on a new energy, as the quiet alleys lead to lively flamenco performances in tucked-away venues, where the raw passion of the dance reverberates against centuries-old walls. It is a neighborhood that invites wandering, where every turn brings a new discovery—an ivy-covered balcony, an artisan's workshop, a centuries-old tavern that seems frozen in time.

There is no single way to explore Santa Cruz; the best way is to simply follow your instincts, let curiosity guide you, and allow yourself to be carried by the rhythm of its streets. It is a place where Seville's soul is most deeply felt, where history lingers not only in the architecture but in the very air itself. In Santa Cruz, the past is not just remembered—it is alive, woven into the fabric of everyday life, waiting to be experienced by those who take the time to listen.

The Riverside Charm of Triana

Across the Guadalquivir River from Seville's historic center lies Triana, a neighborhood that beats with its own rhythm, distinct from the grandeur of the city's main landmarks yet just as essential to Seville's identity. If Santa Cruz is the heart of Seville's history, Triana is its soul—an enclave of flamenco, ceramics, and a fiercely independent spirit that has shaped the city's culture for centuries. It is a neighborhood of storytellers, artisans, and sailors, where the scent of the river mixes with the aroma of sizzling tapas, and where every street corner hums with the echoes of guitars, castanets, and the raw passion of flamenco.

Triana has long been a neighborhood of working-class resilience and artistic brilliance, once home to the city's potters, gypsies, and bullfighters. Its history is woven into the very soil, with ceramic workshops dating back to Moorish times and the famous azulejos—Seville's colorful tiles—bearing the unmistakable mark of Triana's artisans. Even today, the tradition thrives in the small ceramic shops that line Calle Alfarería and Calle San Jorge, where skilled craftsmen shape and paint tiles in the same way their ancestors did centuries ago. These tiles are not just decorations; they are the artistic fingerprint of Seville itself, adorning everything from churches to fountains and even everyday homes.

Walking through Triana, the first thing that catches your eye is the iconic Puente de Triana, the 19th-century iron bridge that connects the neighborhood to the city center. Built over the remains of an older Moorish bridge, it serves as both a literal and symbolic link between Seville's polished grandeur and Triana's raw, unfiltered charm. Crossing the bridge at sunset is an experience in itself, as the golden light reflects off the river, casting a warm glow on the colorful buildings that line the waterfront. This is where Seville feels most alive, with locals gathering along the riverbank, couples strolling hand in hand, and musicians playing for an audience of passersby.

One of the best ways to experience Triana is simply to wander its streets, where life unfolds at an unhurried pace. Plaza del Altozano, the main square at the foot of the bridge, serves as a lively meeting point, with the imposing statue of a torero reminding visitors of the neighborhood's deep connection to bullfighting. From here, the streets lead into a network of alleys and plazas, each revealing something new—a centuries-old chapel, a hidden courtyard, or a bustling tapas bar serving some of the best food in the city. Tapas in Triana are an art form, with neighborhood favorites like Bar Las Golondrinas and Casa Cuesta offering mouthwatering bites of solomillo al whisky (pork in whiskey sauce), crispy fried fish, and garlicky gambas al ajillo.

But above all else, Triana is synonymous with flamenco. This is the birthplace of some of Spain's greatest flamenco singers and dancers, where the art form was nurtured in the humble courtyards and taverns of the neighborhood's past. Even today, the spirit of flamenco is woven into everyday life, with intimate performances found in hidden peñas (flamenco clubs) and small bars where the emotion is raw and the music is unrehearsed. Unlike the tourist shows of the city center, flamenco in Triana is not just a performance—it is a way of life, passed down through generations and felt in every handclap, every foot stomp, and every aching note sung into the night.

Though Triana has modernized in recent years, with trendy bars and boutique hotels emerging alongside its traditional institutions, it has never lost its essence. It remains a place where Seville's soul is most palpable, where the river reflects a neighborhood that has always stood apart, proud of its roots and unafraid to be different. To truly know Seville, you must cross the river, wander its streets, and let Triana work its magic on you. It is not just a place to visit—it is a place to feel, a place to experience, a place to remember.

CHAPTER 3: LANDMARKS AND MUST-SEE ATTRACTIONS

The Magnificent Alcázar of Seville

The Real Alcázar of Seville is not just a palace; it is a masterpiece of history, architecture, and artistry that has stood for more than a thousand years. Walking through its gates is like stepping into a world where Islamic, Gothic, Renaissance, and Baroque influences blend seamlessly, creating a breathtaking testament to the many cultures that have shaped Seville. More than just a monument to the past, the Alcázar is still a living palace, making it the oldest royal residence in Europe still in use. It is a place where history is not merely preserved but felt in every intricate tile, every shaded courtyard, and every whispering fountain.

The story of the Alcázar begins in the days of the Moors, when Muslim rulers constructed a fortress here in the early 10th century. What began as a military stronghold soon evolved into an opulent palace, reflecting the grandeur of Islamic rule in Al-Andalus. When Seville fell to Christian forces in 1248, King Ferdinand III took control of the Alcázar, and over the centuries, Spanish monarchs transformed and expanded it, layering Gothic and Renaissance elements over its Islamic foundations. The result is an architectural wonder where every courtyard, hallway, and garden tells a different chapter of Spain's rich and complex history.

The heart of the Alcázar is the stunning Palacio de Don Pedro, built by King Pedro I in the 14th century. Despite being a Christian ruler, Pedro admired the artistry of Islamic architecture and commissioned Moorish craftsmen to create what is now one of the finest examples of Mudejar design in Spain. As you step into the palace, the intricate beauty of its craftsmanship is overwhelming—delicate stucco carvings, geometric tile patterns, and horseshoe arches adorned with Arabic inscriptions that celebrate the beauty of the universe. The Hall of Ambassadors, the most magnificent room in the palace, is a masterpiece of symmetry, crowned by a golden dome that shimmers in the sunlight. Standing beneath it, one can almost hear the echoes of the royal gatherings, diplomatic meetings, and intrigues that once unfolded here.

Beyond the opulent halls and corridors, the Alcázar's gardens offer a paradise of tranquility. Fountains babble gently beneath towering palm trees, pathways wind through fragrant orange groves, and peacocks strut through the lush greenery as if they, too, are part of the palace's regal history. The gardens are not just decorative; they were designed as a retreat, a place where rulers could escape the heat of Seville's summers and find solace in the harmony of nature. Even today, visitors often find themselves lingering here, lost in the sheer beauty of their surroundings, the scent of jasmine in the air, and the sound of birdsong blending with the soft trickling of water.

Yet, the Alcázar is more than a relic of the past. It is still an official residence of the Spanish royal family, used on special occasions when they visit Seville. Its walls have witnessed everything from medieval battles to modern-day diplomacy, and its influence stretches beyond Spain, having served as an inspiration for countless artists, architects, and even filmmakers. Fans of *Game of Thrones* will recognize it as the stunning setting of Dorne, where its exotic beauty brought to life the fantastical world of the series.

No visit to Seville is complete without experiencing the magic of the Alcázar. Whether marveling at its delicate tilework, wandering through its dreamlike gardens, or simply absorbing the atmosphere of a place that has stood for centuries, one cannot help but feel the weight of history here. It is a place where civilizations converged, where art reached its peak, and where time seems to pause, allowing those who enter to step into a world of unparalleled beauty.

Seville Cathedral and the Giralda

Seville Cathedral is more than just an architectural wonder—it is a monument to ambition, devotion, and the triumph of human ingenuity. Built on the site of a former mosque, this colossal structure stands as one of the largest Gothic cathedrals in the world, a place where the past and present converge in a breathtaking display of art and faith. Its soaring ceilings, intricate altarpieces, and vast interior are designed not just to impress but to overwhelm, leaving visitors in silent awe of its sheer magnitude. Rising beside it is La Giralda, the iconic bell tower that once served as a minaret, standing as a symbol of Seville itself—a city that embraces its Moorish past while standing proudly as a cornerstone of Spanish culture.

The origins of the cathedral date back to the Christian conquest of Seville in 1248 when King Ferdinand III reclaimed the city from Muslim rule. Rather than destroy the existing mosque, the Christians initially converted it into a place of worship. However, in the 15th century, the decision was made to construct an entirely new cathedral—one so grand that, according to legend, the builders declared, "Let us build a church so beautiful and so magnificent that those who see it finished will think we were mad." The result was a structure that defied expectations, a vast masterpiece of Gothic design that took more than a century to complete and remains one of the most awe-inspiring religious buildings in the world.

Stepping inside, the scale is staggering. The cathedral's interior is a vast cavern of stone, illuminated by shafts of colored light filtering through immense stained-glass windows. The Main Chapel, or Capilla Mayor, houses the grand altarpiece, a towering gilded masterpiece that took nearly a century to complete and stands as one of the finest works of religious art in existence. Each panel tells a biblical story, intricately carved and shimmering in gold, drawing the eye upward in an almost hypnotic display of craftsmanship.

Among the cathedral's many treasures is the tomb of Christopher Columbus, a striking monument held aloft by four heraldic figures representing the kingdoms of Castile, León, Aragon, and Navarre. The explorer's remains have traveled nearly as much in death as they did in life, with debates over their authenticity continuing to this day, but for now, he rests here in Seville, the city that played a pivotal role in Spain's Age of Exploration.

But perhaps the greatest experience the cathedral offers is the ascent of La Giralda. Originally built as a minaret in the 12th century during Seville's Islamic rule, it was one of the most advanced architectural feats of its time. When the Christians took control, they preserved the tower, transforming it into a bell tower while maintaining much of its original Moorish design. Unlike traditional staircases, the ascent is made via a series of ramps—a design intended to allow the muezzin to ride a horse to the top for the call to prayer. Today, the climb is a journey through history itself, as each level reveals glimpses of the cathedral's past, while the final steps open onto a panoramic view of Seville that is nothing short of breathtaking. From this vantage point, the city spreads out in all directions, a tapestry of terracotta rooftops, winding streets, and distant church spires, with the Guadalquivir River snaking its way through the urban landscape.

Seville Cathedral and La Giralda are more than just historical landmarks; they are the soul of the city. They embody the grandeur of Seville's past, the artistic genius of its builders, and the enduring faith that shaped its identity. Whether standing beneath the vast Gothic vaults, gazing up at the golden glow of the altarpiece, or taking in the sweeping views from the top of La Giralda, one thing is certain—this is a place that does not merely impress, but moves, inspires, and lingers in the memory long after you have left its sacred walls.

Plaza de España: A Cinematic Marvel

Plaza de España is not just one of Seville's most beautiful landmarks—it is a masterpiece of design, a grand architectural embrace that fuses Spain's diverse influences into a single breathtaking space. Standing within its vast semi-circular sweep, it is impossible not to feel transported, as if you've stepped into a world where history, art, and grandeur converge in perfect harmony. Built for the Ibero-American Exposition of 1929, this plaza was intended to be a showcase of Spain's cultural and artistic legacy, and nearly a century later, it remains one of the most stunning public spaces in the world. With its elegant bridges arching over a Venetian-style canal, its intricate tilework depicting scenes from every Spanish province, and its grand central building adorned with soaring towers, Plaza de España is a place where the past and present meet in an extraordinary setting that feels almost cinematic.

And indeed, it *is* cinematic. The Plaza's sweeping curves, ornate bridges, and majestic towers have made it a sought-after filming location, immortalized in Hollywood films like *Lawrence of Arabia* and *Star Wars: Attack of the Clones*. In George Lucas's vision, this Andalusian gem became the palace city of Theed on the planet Naboo, a fitting transformation for a place that already feels otherworldly in its grandeur. But beyond its moments of cinematic fame, Plaza de España is a living, breathing part of Seville, a place where people gather, musicians perform beneath the arches, and visitors lose themselves in its sheer beauty.

The plaza's architectural brilliance is a reflection of its creator, Aníbal González, who designed it as a celebration of Spanish heritage. The curved shape of the main building symbolizes Spain's open arms, welcoming its former colonies, while the combination of Renaissance, Moorish, and Baroque elements reflects the cultural richness that defines Seville itself. The most striking feature, however, is the elaborate tilework that lines the plaza, a series of alcoves and benches decorated with painted ceramic tiles, each representing a different Spanish province. These azulejos, with their vivid colors and intricate patterns, tell stories of Spain's regional history, creating an open-air museum that invites visitors to explore the country's past one tile at a time.

A stroll through the plaza is an experience of constant discovery. The canal, where visitors can rent rowboats and glide beneath its ornate bridges, adds a touch of romance to the scene, while the towering fountains at the center create a sense of movement and grandeur. The main building, with its arched walkways and elaborate detailing, is a marvel of symmetry and craftsmanship, and climbing its staircases offers stunning views over the entire plaza. Whether you visit in the golden light of morning, when the plaza is quiet and serene, or in the warm glow of sunset, when the sky reflects off its tiled surfaces, there is a timeless magic here that never fades.

More than just an architectural wonder, Plaza de España is the heart of Seville's spirit—grand yet welcoming, historic yet vibrant, a place that belongs as much to the people as it does to history. It is a testament to the city's artistic soul, a space where the past is honored but never frozen in time. Here, history is not just remembered; it is lived, felt, and experienced in every arch, every tile, and every reflection in its waters.

Metropol Parasol: A Modern Wonder

In a city defined by its ancient palaces, Gothic cathedrals, and Moorish courtyards, the Metropol Parasol is a striking contrast—a bold statement of modernity in the heart of historic Seville. Rising above Plaza de la Encarnación like a surreal wooden canopy, this architectural marvel, known locally as *Las Setas* (The Mushrooms), is unlike anything else in the city. It is futuristic, avant-garde, and unapologetically different, a structure that challenges expectations while seamlessly integrating itself into the daily life of Seville.

Designed by the German architect Jürgen Mayer and completed in 2011, the Metropol Parasol is the world's largest wooden structure, its undulating lattice stretching across the plaza like a giant honeycomb of interwoven panels. The design, inspired by the shape of Seville's towering ficus trees and the vaults of the city's Gothic cathedral, is both organic and geometric, a paradox of nature and innovation brought to life through engineering genius. With its six mushroom-like parasols rising above the square, it provides much-needed shade from the relentless Andalusian sun while offering a space that is as functional as it is artistic.

But beyond its sculptural beauty, the Metropol Parasol is an experience. At its base, the underground Antiquarium houses some of Seville's most remarkable Roman and Moorish ruins, discovered during the plaza's excavation and now preserved beneath glass walkways. It is a reminder that even the most futuristic structures in Seville are built upon layers of history. Above ground, the Parasol serves as a lively public space, with markets, restaurants, and events filling the plaza below. But the true magic lies at the top— an undulating walkway that offers one of the most breathtaking panoramic views of Seville. As you ascend via elevator and step onto the curving platform, the city unfolds before you, a sea of terracotta rooftops, bell towers, and distant hills, with La Giralda and the Alcázar standing proudly among them.

Visiting at sunset is an unforgettable experience. The sky shifts from gold to deep orange, then to twilight blue, as Seville glows beneath you, its historic streets winding like veins through the city's heart. At night, the structure itself becomes part of the spectacle, illuminated in soft hues that make it feel even more otherworldly.

While the Metropol Parasol was met with controversy upon its unveiling—many locals initially found its ultra-modern design at odds with Seville's traditional aesthetic—it has since become a beloved landmark, proving that the city's identity is not frozen in time but constantly evolving. It is a place where the past and the future coexist, where ancient ruins and contemporary architecture stand side by side, and where Seville, ever bold, continues to reinvent itself without losing its essence.

To truly understand Seville, one must see both its past and its future. The Metropol Parasol is that future—a daring, innovative, and breathtaking addition to a city that has never been afraid to dream big.

CHAPTER 4: FLAMENCO, FESTIVALS, AND CULTURE

The Soul of Flamenco: Where to Experience It

Flamenco is not just a performance in Seville; it is the beating heart of the city, a raw, passionate expression of its soul. It pulses through the narrow streets of Triana, echoes through the dimly lit tablaos, and rises from the very ground where generations of dancers have stomped, spun, and poured their hearts into the rhythm of the music. To experience flamenco in Seville is to witness something deeply personal, a living tradition that speaks of love, pain, joy, and defiance in ways words never could.

Unlike many forms of entertainment, flamenco is not about polished perfection—it is about feeling. The wail of the *cante* (song) is full of longing, the *toque* (guitar) weaves melodies that seem to cry and sigh, and the *baile* (dance) is an explosion of power and grace, where every stomp and turn carries centuries of history. Flamenco was born from the fusion of cultures—Andalusian, Moorish, Jewish, and Gypsy influences blending to create something unique to southern Spain. And while it has spread across the world, its deepest roots remain in Seville.

There is no shortage of places to experience flamenco here, but the type of show you seek will shape your experience. If you want an intimate, unfiltered glimpse into the rawest form of the art, venture into the *peñas flamencas*—small, often private clubs where locals gather to sing, play, and dance, sometimes spontaneously. These are not choreographed performances for tourists but rather passionate expressions of a tradition passed down through generations. Finding one can be tricky, as many are unadvertised, but asking a local or keeping an ear out for the telltale strumming of a guitar behind a closed door might just lead you to an unforgettable night.

For those looking for a more structured but equally intense performance, Seville's famed tablaos offer breathtaking displays of flamenco at its finest. Venues like *Tablao El Arenal*, *Casa de la Memoria*, and *Los Gallos* are legendary, attracting some of the best dancers and musicians in the country. Here, in intimate settings, the energy is electric, and the performances are mesmerizing, with dancers pouring every ounce of emotion into their movements, the sweat glistening on their foreheads, their feet striking the floor with rhythmic precision that seems almost impossible.

And then there is Triana—the historic flamenco district where the art form grew and flourished. Walking through its streets at night, you can feel its presence in the air. Some of Seville's best flamenco bars, such as *La Carbonería* and *Lo Nuestro*, offer a more relaxed, spontaneous setting where locals and visitors alike come together over drinks, the music flowing as naturally as conversation. It is in places like these where flamenco is at its most authentic—unpredictable, deeply emotional, and utterly spellbinding.

To experience flamenco in Seville is to witness something ancient yet alive, refined yet untamed. It is more than a show; it is a conversation between the past and the present, a story told in song, rhythm, and movement. And when you hear the cry of the singer, feel the pulse of the guitar, and see the fire in the dancer's eyes, you will understand—this is not just music. This is the soul of Seville itself.

Semana Santa and Feria de Abril in 2025

Few cities celebrate tradition with as much passion and spectacle as Seville, and in 2025, the city's two most iconic festivals—Semana Santa and Feria de Abril—promise to be as breathtaking as ever. These events are not mere celebrations; they are the essence of Seville, deeply rooted in its identity, drawing thousands of visitors from across the world to experience their beauty, intensity, and grandeur.

Semana Santa: A Procession of Faith and Devotion

Semana Santa, or Holy Week, is Seville's most solemn and deeply moving event. From Palm Sunday to Easter Sunday, the city transforms into a grand stage of devotion, where centuries-old brotherhoods (*hermandades*) carry massive, ornate floats depicting scenes from the Passion of Christ. The slow, rhythmic beat of drums, the mournful wail of trumpets, and the scent of burning incense fill the air as thousands of hooded penitents (*nazarenos*) march through the historic streets, their candles flickering against the night.

In 2025, Semana Santa will take place from April 13 to April 20, marking a time when Seville becomes a place of reflection, reverence, and overwhelming beauty. The processions move through the city with an almost hypnotic solemnity, and watching them pass—whether in the grandeur of the cathedral, in the narrow alleys of Barrio Santa Cruz, or in the stillness of dawn on *Madrugá*, the most sacred night—is a profoundly emotional experience. The *pasos*, some centuries old, are masterpieces of religious art, carried on the shoulders of the *costaleros* with incredible precision and devotion. Some of the most famous processions, such as *La Macarena* and *El Gran Poder*, draw enormous crowds, and witnessing them is like stepping into a living painting of faith and tradition.

While Semana Santa is primarily a religious event, it is also an artistic and cultural spectacle. The city's balconies fill with onlookers, spontaneous *saetas*—impassioned flamenco-style prayers—are sung from windows, and the atmosphere, though solemn, is deeply communal. For visitors, it is essential to plan ahead, as hotels and streets fill quickly, and securing a good vantage point for the major processions requires patience. But for those who experience it, Semana Santa in Seville is unforgettable—a profound display of devotion that lingers in the heart long after the last candle has burned out.

Feria de Abril: A Week of Pure Joy

Only two weeks after the solemnity of Semana Santa, Seville shifts from deep reflection to pure celebration with the Feria de Abril, the city's most vibrant and extravagant festival. From May 4 to May 10, 2025, the fairgrounds in *Los Remedios* will explode into a world of color, music, and unrestrained joy. The Feria is Seville at its most exuberant—thousands of people dressed in traditional Andalusian attire, horse-drawn carriages parading through the streets, and an endless flow of flamenco, sherry, and dancing that lasts well into the morning hours.

At the heart of the Feria are the *casetas*—private and public tents that line the fairgrounds, each hosting its own celebrations. Inside, families and friends gather to eat, drink, sing, and dance *sevillanas*, the joyful, rhythmic music of

Seville. The Feria is a sensory overload in the best possible way: the scent of fried fish and jamón fills the air, the sound of clapping hands and strumming guitars is everywhere, and the sight of women in dazzling flamenco dresses, their skirts swirling as they dance, is pure Andalusian magic.

The Feria officially begins with the *alumbrao*, the lighting of the grand entrance gate, a spectacle that marks the start of a week of festivities. By day, the fairgrounds are filled with horse parades and traditional Andalusian culture, while at night, the party comes alive with music, dancing, and the infectious energy of thousands of Sevillanos celebrating life. The festivities continue until the grand finale, when fireworks illuminate the Guadalquivir River, closing the Feria with a final burst of beauty.

Visiting Seville during these two festivals is like experiencing two different faces of the same soul—one deeply spiritual, the other joyously uninhibited. Semana Santa moves the heart with its solemn processions, while Feria de Abril sweeps you into a whirlwind of music and dance. Together, they define Seville as a city of tradition, emotion, and passion—a place where every moment, whether of prayer or celebration, is lived to the fullest.

The Art, Music, and Theater Scene

Seville is a city that breathes art, where creativity is woven into its streets, its architecture, and its very identity. This is a place where flamenco rhythms pulse in hidden courtyards, where grand theaters stage operas that have inspired legends, and where the walls of museums whisper stories through canvases drenched in history. The city has long been a muse for poets, painters, and composers, and in 2025, its artistic soul continues to thrive, offering visitors a chance to immerse themselves in a cultural landscape as rich and passionate as the city itself.

A City of Masters: Seville's Fine Art Heritage

Seville's legacy as an artistic powerhouse is undeniable. This is the birthplace of Diego Velázquez, the Baroque master whose works now grace the walls of the world's most prestigious museums. It is also the city that nurtured Bartolomé Esteban Murillo, whose luminous, tender religious paintings helped define Spanish Golden Age art. Their influence lingers in Seville's galleries, particularly in the *Museo de Bellas Artes*, one of Spain's most important art museums. Housed in a former convent, this treasure trove of Spanish painting showcases masterpieces by Murillo, Zurbarán, and Valdés Leal, offering a journey through the artistic evolution of Andalusia.

Beyond the grand masters, Seville continues to foster artistic expression through its contemporary scene. The *Centro Andaluz de Arte Contemporáneo (CAAC)*, set in the stunning surroundings of a former monastery, is a hub for modern and avant-garde art, showcasing thought-provoking exhibitions that challenge and redefine tradition. The city's growing street art movement, particularly in neighborhoods like Alameda and Triana, adds a fresh layer of creativity to Seville's historic landscape, where modern murals sit side by side with centuries-old architecture.

The Music of Seville: From Flamenco to Classical Masterpieces

If there is one art form that defines Seville, it is music. Flamenco is the city's heartbeat, an art of raw emotion that echoes through its tablaos and streets. But beyond flamenco, Seville has played a significant role in the world of classical music and opera. This is the city of *Carmen, Don Giovanni,* and *The Barber of Seville*—operatic masterpieces that have immortalized Seville in song. The *Teatro de la Maestranza,* Seville's grand opera house, continues this legacy, hosting world-class performances ranging from opera to symphony concerts, bringing the works of Verdi, Mozart, and Bizet to life in the city that inspired them.

Seville's musical diversity extends beyond the classical and the traditional. The city's jazz scene thrives in intimate clubs like *Naima Café Jazz,* while contemporary Andalusian musicians blend flamenco with modern influences, creating an ever-evolving soundscape. The annual *Noches en los Jardines del Real Alcázar* offers an extraordinary experience, where music fills the enchanting gardens of the Alcázar, creating a magical fusion of sound and history beneath the stars.

Theater and Performance: A Stage for Every Story

The dramatic spirit of Seville is not confined to its operas and flamenco stages. Theater is an integral part of the city's cultural fabric, from grand historic venues to intimate experimental spaces. The *Teatro Lope de Vega,* an architectural gem built for the 1929 Ibero-American Exposition, is the city's premier venue for drama, dance, and live performance, hosting everything from Spanish Golden Age plays to contemporary productions.

For those seeking an alternative, the *Sala Cero Teatro* and *Teatro Central* offer a more experimental experience, showcasing innovative performances that push artistic boundaries. Seville's street theater scene is also worth exploring—during festivals and cultural events, the city's plazas and alleyways transform into open-air stages where performances unfold beneath the Andalusian sky.

Art as a Way of Life

In Seville, art is not something locked away in museums or confined to theaters; it is everywhere. It is in the intricate tiles of the Alcázar, the poetry of García Lorca whispered in bookshops, the impassioned verses of a flamenco song, and the sweeping gestures of a dancer lost in the rhythm of the *compás*. This is a city where creativity is not just celebrated—it is lived, felt, and breathed in every moment. And in 2025, whether you come to admire the masterpieces of the past or to discover the voices shaping the future, Seville's art scene promises to captivate, inspire, and leave you spellbound.

CHAPTER 5: A TASTE OF SEVILLE

Tapas Culture: What to Eat and Where

Seville is a city where food is not just a necessity but a way of life, and nowhere is this more evident than in its tapas culture. Tapas are more than just small plates; they are a social ritual, an invitation to linger, to sip, to savor, and to enjoy the slow rhythm of Andalusian life. To eat tapas in Seville is to embark on a culinary adventure where every bite tells a story—of history, tradition, and the vibrant soul of the city. In 2025, the tapas scene is as strong as ever, blending time-honored classics with bold new interpretations, all served in atmospheric bars that range from century-old taverns to sleek modern gastropubs.

The Essence of Tapas: A Way of Eating, Not Just a Dish

Unlike a traditional sit-down meal, tapas are meant to be shared and enjoyed at a leisurely pace, often while standing at a crowded bar, chatting with friends, and hopping from one venue to the next. In Seville, the best way to experience tapas is the way the locals do—by going on a *tapeo*, a tapas crawl, where you move from bar to bar, sampling a specialty at each stop. Whether it's a crispy *croqueta*, a tender slice of Iberian ham, or a sizzling plate of *gambas al ajillo*, each tapa is a new discovery, a new expression of Seville's rich culinary heritage.

What to Eat: Classic Tapas You Can't Miss

Seville's tapas scene is built on centuries of culinary tradition, with recipes passed down through generations and perfected over time. Some dishes are essential to any tapas experience, offering a taste of the city's history in every bite.

A good starting point is *jamón ibérico de bellota*, the king of Spanish ham, cured for years and meltingly rich with nutty undertones. Another staple is *queso manchego*, a firm, aged cheese that pairs beautifully with a glass of local sherry. Fried foods are a Sevillian specialty, and few things are more satisfying than *pescaíto frito*—an assortment of lightly battered and perfectly crisp fried fish, best eaten with a squeeze of fresh lemon.

For a taste of Seville's Moorish past, try *espinacas con garbanzos*, a comforting dish of slow-cooked spinach and chickpeas seasoned with cumin and paprika. Another must-try is *solomillo al whisky*, pork tenderloin bathed in a rich whiskey and garlic sauce, a dish that has become a signature of the city's traditional bars. If you want something truly Sevillian, order *carrillada de cerdo*, succulent braised pork cheeks slow-cooked in red wine until they fall apart with the touch of a fork.

Of course, no tapas experience is complete without *tortilla de patatas*, Spain's beloved potato omelet, and *patatas bravas*, crispy fried potatoes topped with a spicy tomato sauce and creamy aioli. And for seafood lovers, *gambas al ajillo*—prawns sizzling in garlic-infused olive oil—delivers simple perfection in every bite.

Where to Eat: The Best Tapas Bars in Seville

Seville is a city of countless tapas bars, each with its own specialty and personality. Some are historic institutions, where generations have gathered over plates of *montaditos* (small sandwiches) and glasses of *fino* sherry, while others are modern interpretations, offering creative twists on classic dishes.

For a taste of history, *El Rinconcillo* is the oldest bar in Seville, dating back to 1670. Here, amidst dark wooden beams and hanging legs of ham, you can sip a glass of dry sherry and enjoy traditional tapas like *espinacas con garbanzos* and *bacalao frito* (fried cod). Another legendary spot is *Casa Morales*, where huge clay wine barrels line the walls and the atmosphere is as authentically Sevillian as it gets.

For the best Iberian ham, head to *Casa Román*, nestled in the heart of Barrio Santa Cruz, where wafer-thin slices of *jamón ibérico* are cut by hand and served with rustic bread. Meanwhile, *Bodeguita Romero* is famous for its *montadito de pringá*, a small but mighty sandwich packed with slow-cooked meats and bursting with flavor.

If you're looking for a more modern take on tapas, *Eslava* is a must-visit, with award-winning dishes like their *huevo sobre bizcocho de boletus*, a delicate soft-boiled egg served on a mushroom cake. *La Brunilda*, another favorite, offers beautifully presented tapas with contemporary flair, from seared tuna with soy glaze to tender beef cheeks in red wine sauce.

For those who love seafood, *Freiduría La Isla* is a classic choice for crispy fried fish, while *La Azotea* is renowned for its inventive seafood dishes, from razor clams with garlic to perfectly grilled octopus.

The Perfect Pairing: What to Drink with Your Tapas

A great tapas experience is not just about the food—it's also about what you drink alongside it. Seville is in the heart of Andalusia, making it the perfect place to sample the region's iconic wines. A glass of dry *fino* or *manzanilla* sherry pairs beautifully with ham and seafood, while a robust *rioja* or *ribera del duero* red wine complements heartier dishes like *carrillada*.

Beer is also a favorite choice among locals, with *Cruzcampo*, Seville's homegrown lager, being the drink of choice at most bars. And if you want to cool off on a warm evening, a refreshing *tinto de verano*—red wine mixed with soda and ice—is the perfect way to sip your way through the city's tapas culture.

A Culinary Experience to Remember

Eating tapas in Seville is more than just a meal—it's an experience, a tradition, and a way to connect with the city's spirit. It is about squeezing into a lively bar, watching the bartender scribble your order in chalk on the counter, and discovering flavors that have stood the test of time. Whether you stick to the classics or explore the city's modern gastronomic innovations, one thing is certain: Seville's tapas culture is an unforgettable journey, one delicious bite at a time.

Traditional Andalusian Dishes You Must Try

Seville's cuisine is a reflection of its history, a melting pot of flavors shaped by centuries of Roman, Moorish, and Spanish influences. Andalusian food is deeply rooted in tradition, with dishes that have been passed down through generations, each bite carrying the essence of the land, the sun, and the sea. To truly experience Seville, you must indulge in its most iconic dishes—recipes that tell the story of Andalusia through their ingredients, their preparation, and the passion with which they are served. In 2025, Seville continues to honor its culinary heritage, while also embracing innovation, making it an exciting time to discover the flavors that define this vibrant city.

One of the most beloved Andalusian dishes is *gazpacho*, a chilled tomato soup that is the ultimate refreshment on a hot Sevillian day. Made with ripe tomatoes, peppers, cucumbers, garlic, olive oil, and vinegar, gazpacho is light, fresh, and deeply satisfying. Its cousin, *salmorejo*, is a thicker, creamier variation, enriched with bread and often topped with chopped hard-boiled eggs and Iberian ham. While both soups share similar ingredients, salmorejo's velvety texture and richer taste make it a favorite among locals, particularly as a starter before a main course.

For a heartier option, *rabo de toro* (oxtail stew) is a dish that speaks of Seville's deep-rooted bullfighting tradition. This slow-cooked delicacy dates back to the 16th century and is prepared with tender oxtail braised in red wine, tomatoes, and aromatic spices until it falls off the bone. Rich, flavorful, and deeply comforting, rabo de toro is best enjoyed with a glass of full-bodied red wine and a side of crusty bread to soak up the sauce.

Another staple of Andalusian cuisine is *flamenquín*, a golden-fried roll of pork loin stuffed with ham and cheese, coated in breadcrumbs, and deep-fried to crispy perfection. Originally from Córdoba but beloved throughout Andalusia, flamenquín is a satisfying combination of textures—crunchy on the outside, tender and melty on the inside. A perfect choice for those looking for a decadent bite of traditional Andalusian indulgence.

Seville is also known for its love of seafood, and *pescaíto frito* (fried fish) is one of the city's most iconic dishes. Small fish such as anchovies, cuttlefish, or baby squid are lightly coated in flour and fried in olive oil until crisp, creating a simple yet incredibly flavorful dish. It is best eaten piping hot, with just a squeeze of fresh lemon, ideally while sitting in a lively bar near the Guadalquivir River. If you want to take it a step further, *puntillitas*—tiny fried squid—or *boquerones en vinagre*, fresh anchovies marinated in vinegar, garlic, and parsley, are must-tries for seafood lovers.

For a dish with Moorish origins, *berenjenas con miel* (fried eggplant with honey) is a delightful combination of savory and sweet, inspired by the culinary traditions left behind by Andalusia's Islamic past. Thin slices of eggplant are fried until golden and drizzled with cane honey, creating an irresistible contrast between the crispy, slightly salty eggplant and the rich sweetness of the honey. It's a perfect example of how Seville's food reflects its layered history, blending flavors from different cultures into something uniquely Andalusian.

If you're in search of a comforting, home-style dish, *espinacas con garbanzos* (spinach with chickpeas) is a humble yet deeply flavorful option that has been a staple in Seville for centuries. Cooked with garlic, paprika, cumin, and sometimes a touch of vinegar, this simple but satisfying dish is a favorite during Semana Santa but can be enjoyed year-round in traditional tapas bars. Pair it with a glass of dry sherry, and you have a truly authentic Sevillian experience.

For meat lovers, *solomillo al whisky* is one of the city's signature dishes. This mouthwatering pork tenderloin is cooked in a rich garlic and whiskey sauce, creating a deeply aromatic dish that pairs beautifully with fried potatoes. A staple of many traditional tapas bars, this dish is a prime example of how simple ingredients, when combined with skill and tradition, can produce something truly unforgettable.

No exploration of Andalusian cuisine would be complete without a taste of *tortillitas de camarones*, delicate shrimp fritters that hail from the coastal regions of Cádiz but are widely loved in Seville. Made with a chickpea and wheat flour batter, tiny shrimp, parsley, and onion, these paper-thin fritters are fried until golden and crisp, offering a bite that is light, airy, and packed with seafood flavor.

And finally, for those with a sweet tooth, *tocino de cielo* is one of Seville's most famous desserts. This rich egg yolk flan, created by nuns centuries ago, is a decadent, silky treat that melts in your mouth, with a caramelized top that adds the perfect touch of sweetness. If you prefer something lighter, *pestiños*—honey-glazed fried dough flavored with orange and anise—are a traditional Andalusian treat enjoyed especially during Easter and Christmas.

Eating in Seville is an experience that goes beyond the food itself. It is about tradition, history, and the joy of sharing a meal in good company. Whether you find yourself in a centuries-old tavern or a bustling market stall, each dish tells a story, each flavor speaks of Andalusia's rich past, and every bite invites you to savor the heart and soul of Seville.

The Best Rooftop Bars and Cafés

Seville is a city best experienced from above, where the golden rooftops, intricate church spires, and the winding Guadalquivir River create a breathtaking panorama that shifts with the light of day. Whether it's the warm glow of sunset reflecting off the Giralda, the soft hum of the city at night, or the gentle morning breeze rolling over terracotta tiles, Seville's rooftop bars and cafés offer an unparalleled way to soak in its beauty. In 2025, these elevated escapes continue to be some of the most sought-after spots in the city, combining stunning views with exquisite drinks, gourmet tapas, and the unmistakable charm of Andalusian hospitality.

For those who want to sip a cocktail while gazing at the magnificent Seville Cathedral, *La Terraza de EME* is a must-visit. Perched atop the stylish EME Catedral Hotel, this bar offers front-row seats to one of the most iconic views in the city. The Giralda, illuminated against the twilight sky, feels close enough to touch, making it the perfect place for a romantic evening or a celebratory toast. The menu features expertly crafted cocktails, from classic gin and tonics to innovative blends inspired by Andalusian flavors, as well as a refined selection of wines and spirits. It's a glamorous spot where the atmosphere is as intoxicating as the drinks.

If you're looking for something a little more relaxed but still with breathtaking views, *Pura Vida Terraza* is an excellent choice. Located on the rooftop of Hotel Fontecruz, this laid-back terrace blends chill vibes with a prime location. The view of the Cathedral is stunning, but what makes this spot unique is its focus on live music, particularly flamenco. On select evenings, you can sip a glass of wine while listening to the soulful strumming of a Spanish guitar, letting the magic of Seville wash over you.

For a rooftop experience that captures the essence of Triana's charm, *Mariatrifulca* is the place to be. While not a traditional rooftop, this terrace sits on the banks of the Guadalquivir, offering a mesmerizing perspective of the river, the Puente de Triana, and the lively movement of boats and people passing below. Known for its exceptional seafood and Mediterranean dishes, this restaurant-bar is perfect for a long, indulgent evening of dining under the stars. Order a plate of *gambas al ajillo* or *tuna tartare* and pair it with a crisp glass of *manzanilla* sherry for a truly Sevillian experience.

If what you seek is an exclusive and modern take on rooftop culture, *Hotel Doña María's Terraza* is another unbeatable option. Nestled in the heart of the city, this rooftop bar has been a favorite among locals and travelers alike for its vibrant atmosphere and sweeping views of Seville's skyline. The ambiance here is a mix of chic and casual, making it an ideal place for an aperitif before heading out for a night of flamenco or tapas hopping. With a signature cocktail list that includes refreshing blends infused with Andalusian citrus and local herbs, it's a stylish retreat from the bustling streets below.

For those who appreciate a more bohemian touch, *La Terraza de los Seises* offers a charming mix of history and elegance. This rooftop café, located in the Casa de los Seises hotel, combines a relaxed, welcoming atmosphere with an incredible view of the Cathedral. During the day, it's the perfect spot for a quiet coffee while soaking up the sunshine, while in the evening, it transforms into an intimate cocktail lounge with soft lighting and a gentle breeze that makes the city feel even more enchanting.

If you prefer something away from the tourist-heavy areas, *Rooftop Albarama* is a hidden gem that blends modern aesthetics with Andalusian warmth. Overlooking Plaza Nueva, this elegant yet unpretentious terrace is ideal for those who want to enjoy high-quality tapas with a contemporary twist while taking in a different side of the city's skyline. Their menu includes gourmet versions of classic Andalusian dishes, such as Iberian pork with whiskey sauce and delicately prepared seafood specialties.

For those who want a rooftop experience with a truly local touch, *El Corte Inglés Gourmet Experience* is a lesser-known but fantastic option. Located atop Seville's iconic department store, this rooftop offers not only an incredible view of the city but also a curated selection of the finest Andalusian and Spanish cuisine. Whether you want to sample aged Iberian ham, fresh oysters, or a selection of local wines, this spot is a paradise for food lovers who want to enjoy panoramic views while indulging in high-quality flavors.

Rooftop culture in Seville is more than just about the view— it's about capturing the spirit of the city from a new perspective. It's about feeling the cool evening air while savoring the last golden light of the day, clinking glasses against the backdrop of history, and letting the rhythms of

Seville carry you through the night. Whether you're here for a romantic getaway, a night out with friends, or a quiet moment above the city's lively streets, these rooftops offer an experience that is as unforgettable as the city itself.

CHAPTER 6: BEYOND THE CITY: DAY TRIPS AND EXCURSIONS

Córdoba and the Mesmerizing Mezquita

A visit to Seville is never complete without a journey to Córdoba, a city where history whispers from every archway, courtyard, and cobblestone street. Though just a short train ride away, Córdoba feels like stepping into a different world—one where the echoes of Al-Andalus still linger in the air, where jasmine-scented patios burst with color, and where the breathtaking Mezquita, one of the most extraordinary architectural wonders in the world, stands as a testament to the city's layered past.

Córdoba was once the dazzling capital of the Umayyad Caliphate, a city of scholars, poets, and philosophers, where knowledge flourished in the grandest libraries of medieval Europe. During its golden age, it was the most advanced city on the continent, a beacon of learning and culture where Muslims, Christians, and Jews coexisted and contributed to its intellectual brilliance. Today, that spirit is still palpable, particularly in the labyrinthine streets of the old town, where Roman bridges, Moorish palaces, and Renaissance churches create a seamless blend of civilizations.

The Mezquita-Catedral, or the Great Mosque of Córdoba, is the crown jewel of the city, a masterpiece that captures the essence of Andalucía's rich history. The moment you step inside, you are enveloped by a mesmerizing sea of red-and-white horseshoe arches, an endless forest of columns that stretch in perfect symmetry, creating an atmosphere that is at once intimate and awe-inspiring. Built in the 8th century on the site of a Visigothic church, the Mezquita was once the most magnificent mosque in the Western Islamic world, a place of worship that reflected the grandeur of Al-Andalus.

As you wander through its vast interior, the air thick with history, you will notice the seamless fusion of Islamic and Christian artistry. In the 16th century, after the Reconquista, a grand Catholic cathedral was inserted into the heart of the mosque, an architectural paradox that still sparks wonder and debate. The soaring nave, ornate altars, and Baroque embellishments rise dramatically within the Moorish framework, creating a contrast that is both stunning and surreal. It is a place where past and present exist side by side, where the echoes of Muslim prayers seem to blend with the sound of ringing church bells.

Outside the Mezquita, the *Patio de los Naranjos* offers a moment of tranquility. This courtyard, filled with fragrant orange trees and ancient fountains, was once the site of ablutions before prayer. Today, it is a peaceful oasis where visitors pause to reflect, shaded by the same trees that have watched over Córdoba for centuries. Step beyond its walls, and you will find yourself in the heart of the Jewish Quarter, one of the most enchanting parts of the city.

The Judería, as it is known, is a maze of narrow, whitewashed streets adorned with blue flowerpots, leading to hidden courtyards and centuries-old synagogues. One of the few remaining medieval synagogues in Spain, the *Sinagoga de Córdoba*, is a small yet poignant reminder of the city's Jewish heritage. The Calleja de las Flores, one of the most photographed spots in Córdoba, offers a postcard-perfect glimpse of the Mezquita framed by cascading blooms and rustic Andalusian charm.

Córdoba is also famous for its *patios*, an art form in themselves. Each spring, during the *Fiesta de los Patios*, the city bursts into a riot of color as locals open their homes to showcase their stunning courtyard gardens, filled with overflowing geraniums, azaleas, and bougainvillea. Even outside of festival season, many patios remain open to the public, offering a glimpse into a tradition that has defined Córdoba's architectural soul for centuries.

No visit to Córdoba is complete without indulging in its culinary delights. The city's signature dish, *salmorejo*, is a richer, creamier cousin of gazpacho—made with ripe tomatoes, garlic, olive oil, and bread, then topped with Iberian ham and hard-boiled eggs. Pair it with a glass of Montilla-Moriles wine, a local sherry-like variety, and you have the perfect Andalusian meal. For something heartier, *rabo de toro* (oxtail stew) is a must-try, a dish that dates back to Córdoba's bullfighting traditions and is slow-cooked to perfection.

As you wander back toward the Roman Bridge, with the warm glow of sunset reflecting off the Guadalquivir River, you will understand why Córdoba remains one of Spain's most captivating cities. It is a place where every stone has a story, where cultures have intertwined for centuries, and where history is not just preserved—it is felt. Whether you come for a day or choose to linger longer, Córdoba and its mesmerizing Mezquita will leave an imprint on your soul, a reminder that Andalucía is a land where the past is always present, waiting to be discovered anew.

Jerez de la Frontera: Wine and Equestrian Beauty

Jerez de la Frontera, often simply called Jerez, is a city where tradition and elegance intertwine, creating an experience that is both deeply Andalusian and uniquely its own. Just an hour south of Seville, Jerez is famous for two things that define its character: sherry wine and the noble art of equestrian mastery. A visit here is an immersion into a world where vineyards stretch across sun-drenched hills, where the rhythmic sound of trotting Andalusian horses echoes through historic courtyards, and where the air is perfumed with the scent of aged oak barrels and orange blossoms.

Wine is the lifeblood of Jerez, and its most celebrated creation, sherry, has captivated palates for centuries. Unlike any other wine, sherry is crafted through a unique aging process called the *solera* system, where younger wines blend with older ones in stacked barrels, creating complex layers of flavor that range from bone-dry *fino* to rich, caramel-hued *oloroso*. The best way to understand this alchemy is to visit one of the city's legendary bodegas. At González Byass, home to the world-famous *Tío Pepe*, visitors can walk among towering casks, each marked with the signatures of famous figures who have passed through. At Bodegas Lustau, sherry tasting becomes an art, with sommeliers guiding you through the subtle nuances of each variety, from the crisp almond notes of *manzanilla* to the deep, nutty richness of *Pedro Ximénez*. Every sip tells a story of sun-drenched vineyards, Atlantic breezes, and centuries-old craftsmanship.

But Jerez is not just about wine—it is also the cradle of one of Spain's most cherished equestrian traditions. The city is home to the Royal Andalusian School of Equestrian Art, where the majestic Andalusian horses, known for their grace and strength, perform a breathtaking ballet of precise movements and sheer power. Watching these horses in action is witnessing centuries of training and tradition unfold before your eyes. The *Cómo Bailan los Caballos Andaluces* (How the Andalusian Horses Dance) show is a mesmerizing display of classical dressage, where riders in 18th-century costumes guide their steeds through intricate, almost dance-like maneuvers to the sound of Spanish guitar. It is an experience that speaks to the deep connection between Andalusians and their horses, a bond forged over generations.

Beyond its wine and equestrian heritage, Jerez is a city of charm and history. The Alcázar of Jerez, a Moorish fortress dating back to the 11th century, stands as a reminder of the city's Islamic past. Within its walls, visitors can explore a beautifully preserved mosque, elegant gardens, and the old olive oil mill, offering a glimpse into life during the days of Al-Andalus. From its rooftop, the views stretch over the rooftops of the old town, where the golden dome of the Cathedral of Jerez rises above the skyline. This imposing Baroque structure, built atop a former mosque, is an architectural marvel in itself, blending Gothic, Renaissance, and Neoclassical elements in a stunning display of Andalusian grandeur.

The rhythm of Jerez is not just in the hooves of its horses or the pouring of its sherry—it is also in its music. This city is one of the birthplaces of *flamenco*, and its streets seem to pulse with its raw, passionate energy. In the intimate *tabancos*—traditional flamenco bars hidden among the winding alleys—locals and visitors alike gather to witness performances that are as fiery as they are soulful. Places like *Tabanco El Pasaje* and *La Guarida del Ángel* offer an authentic flamenco experience, where the singers' voices crack with emotion, the guitarists weave intricate melodies, and the dancers stomp and twirl with an intensity that is impossible to forget.

Of course, no trip to Jerez would be complete without indulging in its local cuisine. The city's gastronomy is deeply tied to its wine culture, with dishes that pair perfectly with the many varieties of sherry. A plate of *jamón ibérico* alongside a chilled glass of *fino* is a must, as is the local specialty, *berza jerezana*—a hearty stew of chickpeas, chorizo, and cabbage. And for something truly unique, try *langostinos de Sanlúcar*, the delicate prawns from nearby Sanlúcar de Barrameda, best enjoyed with a glass of crisp, sea-breeze-infused *manzanilla*.

As the sun sets over the whitewashed courtyards and vine-covered patios of Jerez, the city's magic becomes undeniable. Whether you have come for the sherry, the horses, the flamenco, or simply the allure of Andalucía's hidden gems, Jerez de la Frontera offers an experience that lingers long after you leave. It is a place where time slows, where tradition is cherished, and where every glass of wine, every note of music, and every elegant movement of a horse tells a story of centuries past and present.

Doñana National Park: A Natural Wonderland

Doñana National Park is one of Spain's most treasured natural landscapes, a breathtaking expanse where vast wetlands, shifting dunes, and ancient forests come together to create an ecological wonderland unlike any other. Nestled between the provinces of Seville, Huelva, and Cádiz, this UNESCO-listed biosphere is not just a refuge for wildlife but a place where nature unfolds in its purest form, untouched and untamed. It is a land of contrasts—one moment you're gazing out at sweeping marshlands teeming with flamingos, the next you're surrounded by golden sand dunes that stretch endlessly toward the horizon. Every season brings a transformation, making Doñana a living, breathing testament to the beauty and resilience of the natural world.

What makes Doñana truly remarkable is its role as a sanctuary for migratory birds. Sitting at the crossroads of Europe and Africa, it serves as a critical stopover for thousands of birds that journey between the continents, seeking rest and sustenance in its rich wetlands. In spring and autumn, the skies come alive with the spectacle of birds in motion—graceful herons, elegant egrets, and flocks of flamingos painting the shallow waters with their unmistakable pink hues. For birdwatchers, it is paradise, a place where every turn reveals another marvel, whether it's the haunting call of a spoonbill or the swift movement of a kingfisher skimming across the water.

But Doñana is more than just a haven for birds. It is also home to some of Spain's most elusive and endangered species, including the majestic Iberian lynx. This rare and beautiful feline, with its tufted ears and piercing eyes, is one of the most endangered wild cats in the world, yet here, in the dense Mediterranean forests of Doñana, it still roams free. Spotting one is a matter of patience and luck, but knowing that such a creature still exists in the wild adds an air of mystery to the park. Alongside the lynx, the Iberian imperial eagle soars overhead, while wild boars, red deer, and even the occasional mongoose make their way through the undergrowth.

The landscapes of Doñana are as varied as its wildlife. The park is a mosaic of ecosystems, each with its own distinct character and charm. The *Marismas*, or marshlands, are the heart of Doñana, vast wetlands that flood in winter and become an oasis for wildlife. When the rains come, the land transforms into a shimmering lake, reflecting the sky and attracting thousands of birds that wade through its waters. As the seasons shift, the marshes dry, revealing a cracked, otherworldly terrain where birds pick their way through the mud, searching for the last remnants of water. Then there are the *cotos*, the forests of umbrella pines and cork oaks that provide shade and shelter for many of the park's land-dwelling creatures. Walking through these woodlands feels like stepping into a fairytale, where the scent of pine lingers in the air, and the stillness is broken only by the occasional rustle of wildlife in the underbrush.

Perhaps the most striking feature of Doñana, however, is its *dunas móviles*—the great moving sand dunes that shift with the winds, reshaping the landscape year after year. These towering dunes, sculpted by time and weather, are constantly in motion, swallowing forests and creating new terrains in an endless cycle of change. Walking across them, with the Atlantic breeze in your hair and the endless stretch of sand beneath your feet, is an experience that reminds you of nature's power and unpredictability.

Exploring Doñana is an adventure in itself, and while much of the park is protected and requires guided tours, there are plenty of ways to experience its magic. Jeep safaris take visitors deep into the wilderness, where experienced guides lead you through its many ecosystems, sharing stories of its wildlife and history. Boat tours along the Guadalquivir River offer a different perspective, gliding past the marshes as birds take flight in the golden light of sunset. For those who prefer a quieter experience, hiking trails wind through the edges of the park, leading to breathtaking viewpoints and hidden corners where the wild truly feels untouched.

A visit to Doñana is incomplete without stopping by El Rocío, the picturesque village that feels like a place frozen in time. With its sandy, unpaved streets and whitewashed houses, it is famous for the annual *Romería del Rocío*, a massive pilgrimage that draws thousands of devotees from across Spain. But even outside the festival, the town exudes a unique charm, with horse-drawn carriages clattering through its streets and the serene beauty of the marshlands visible from its edges.

Doñana National Park is more than just a destination; it is a reminder of the wild, untamed beauty that still exists in the world. Whether you come for the birds, the lynx, the landscapes, or simply to lose yourself in nature's grandeur, it is a place that stays with you long after you've left. In a world where wilderness is disappearing, Doñana stands as a testament to the power of preservation, a living masterpiece of nature that continues to inspire and awe.

Getting Around: Public Transport and Walking Routes

Seville is a city best experienced at a leisurely pace, where every street, plaza, and hidden alleyway holds a piece of history or a glimpse of everyday life. While the city's layout is compact and walkable, it also has a well-connected public transportation system that makes getting around seamless, whether you're exploring the grand boulevards of the historic center or venturing into the vibrant neighborhoods beyond. Understanding the best ways to navigate Seville will help you make the most of your time in this enchanting city.

Walking is undoubtedly the most rewarding way to experience Seville. The city's historic core, with its labyrinthine streets and stunning landmarks, is largely pedestrian-friendly, encouraging visitors to take their time and soak in the atmosphere. Strolling through the charming Barrio Santa Cruz, wandering past the awe-inspiring Seville Cathedral, or meandering along the picturesque Guadalquivir River allows you to fully appreciate the city's architecture, street life, and small details that might otherwise go unnoticed. The scent of orange blossoms in spring, the sound of flamenco guitar echoing from a hidden courtyard, or the sight of a spontaneous procession winding through a narrow street—these are moments that can only be discovered on foot.

For longer distances or to give your feet a break, Seville's public transport offers several convenient options. The *Metro de Sevilla* is a single-line metro system that runs from the southern outskirts of the city to the western neighborhoods, passing through key areas such as San Bernardo and Prado de San Sebastián. While it may not be the most extensive metro system, it is a quick and efficient way to move across town when needed.

The city's *tranvía*, or tram, is a charming and practical way to travel through the heart of Seville. The *MetroCentro* tram line connects Plaza Nueva, near the Cathedral, to San Bernardo, passing by major points of interest such as the Archivo de Indias, the University of Seville, and Prado de San Sebastián. The tram is especially useful for those wanting a quick ride between the main attractions without having to navigate the sometimes confusing bus routes.

Buses are the most comprehensive public transport option, covering nearly every corner of the city. Operated by *TUSSAM*, the bus network is reliable and affordable, with routes running throughout the day and into the late evening. Key lines for visitors include the *C3* and *C4*, which loop around the historic center, and the *EA* airport bus, which connects the city center with Seville Airport. For those staying in more residential areas or exploring beyond the tourist hotspots, buses are an excellent way to get around.

Cycling has also become increasingly popular in Seville, thanks to its extensive network of bike lanes and the city's *Sevici* bike-sharing program. With stations spread throughout the city, *Sevici* offers an eco-friendly and enjoyable way to explore at your own pace. Cycling along the riverfront or through Maria Luisa Park is particularly scenic, providing a refreshing alternative to navigating the bustling streets on foot.

For a more traditional way to experience the city, horse-drawn carriages, known as *coches de caballos*, remain a picturesque and leisurely option. While often seen as a tourist attraction, these carriages offer a unique perspective of Seville's historic beauty, especially when taken in the evening as the city lights reflect off its grand monuments.

Taxis and rideshare services like Uber and Cabify are readily available, making it easy to get to destinations that may be less accessible by public transport. While taxis can be hailed on the street or found at designated stands near major landmarks, using an app ensures clear pricing and the convenience of requesting a ride from anywhere.

For those looking to explore beyond the city, Seville's Santa Justa train station provides high-speed rail connections to destinations such as Córdoba, Madrid, and Málaga. The *Cercanías* commuter trains also offer convenient routes to nearby towns and attractions, making day trips effortless.

Navigating Seville is part of the adventure, whether you're walking through its storied streets, hopping on a tram, or cycling past its grand plazas. However you choose to explore, the city's transport options ensure that every journey, no matter how short or long, is filled with the charm and beauty that make Seville so unforgettable.

Where to Stay: From Boutique Hotels to Budget Stays

Seville offers a wide range of accommodations, each reflecting the city's vibrant character, rich history, and warm Andalusian hospitality. Whether you're looking for a luxurious boutique hotel housed in a centuries-old palace, a stylish modern stay with rooftop views, or a budget-friendly guesthouse that doesn't compromise on charm, Seville has something for every traveler. Choosing where to stay depends on your style, budget, and how you want to experience the city—from the romance of historic quarters to the convenience of more contemporary districts.

For those seeking an immersive experience in Seville's old-world charm, the historic center is an unbeatable choice. Staying in Barrio Santa Cruz, the city's former Jewish quarter, means waking up to narrow, winding streets, hidden courtyards filled with orange trees, and the echoes of flamenco drifting from tucked-away taverns. Boutique hotels here often occupy former mansions, such as the exquisite Hotel Casa 1800, where 19th-century elegance meets modern comfort, or the romantic Corral del Rey, known for its intimate atmosphere and stunning rooftop terrace. The advantage of staying in this area is that you are just steps away from the Seville Cathedral, the Alcázar, and the picturesque Plaza de Doña Elvira, making it perfect for those who want to soak in the city's beauty from dawn until dusk.

The Arenal district, nestled between the historic center and the Guadalquivir River, offers another fantastic location, especially for those who enjoy being close to cultural landmarks and lively nightlife. This area is home to some of Seville's most refined accommodations, such as the Hotel Mercer Sevilla, where contemporary design meets Andalusian tradition, and the EME Catedral Hotel, which boasts a rooftop pool with breathtaking views of the Giralda. Staying in Arenal also places you near the Plaza de Toros, the Maestranza Theatre, and some of the city's best tapas bars, ensuring that your evenings are just as memorable as your days.

For travelers who prefer a more local and artistic vibe, Triana is an excellent choice. Across the river from the historic center, this traditional neighborhood is known for its ceramic workshops, flamenco heritage, and authentic Andalusian atmosphere. Hotels here tend to be more relaxed and often come with a more residential feel. The Zenit Sevilla offers comfort and style with a rooftop terrace overlooking the city, while the charming Boutique Hotel Triana provides a cozy retreat with a touch of Sevillian authenticity. Staying in Triana means you'll experience a different side of Seville, one where the mornings are filled with the scent of fresh churros and evenings are spent in lively taverns where locals gather for music and conversation.

For those who enjoy modern luxury and sleek design, the Nervión district, just outside the historic center, offers contemporary hotels with excellent amenities. This area is ideal for business travelers or those looking for a quieter stay while remaining well-connected to the main attractions. Hotels such as the Meliá Sevilla and the NH Collection Sevilla offer spacious rooms, swimming pools, and proximity to the stunning Plaza de España and Maria Luisa Park. Nervión is also home to one of Seville's main shopping districts, making it a great option for those who want to indulge in retail therapy between sightseeing adventures.

Budget-conscious travelers will find plenty of options that provide comfort without breaking the bank. The Alfalfa neighborhood, just northeast of the Cathedral, is a great area for budget-friendly stays, offering a mix of charming guesthouses and lively hostels. The For You Hostel Sevilla is a popular choice among backpackers, combining stylish dorms with a friendly atmosphere, while Pension Córdoba offers simple yet charming rooms in a historic Sevillian house. Hostels like The Nomad Hostel & Café are also great for solo travelers looking to meet others, with communal spaces and organized activities that encourage socializing.

No matter where you stay in Seville, the city's charm is never far away. Whether you choose a luxurious hotel with rooftop views of the Giralda, a traditional guesthouse in a flower-filled courtyard, or a trendy boutique stay in a vibrant neighborhood, each accommodation adds to the experience of discovering Seville's magic. The key is finding the place that best suits your style, ensuring that every moment—from waking up in the heart of the city to returning after a night of tapas and flamenco—is as enchanting as the city itself.

Money, Safety, and Local Etiquette

Navigating the practical aspects of Seville will ensure a smooth and enjoyable experience, allowing you to focus on the magic of the city without unnecessary worries. Understanding how money works, keeping safety in mind, and respecting local etiquette will help you blend in seamlessly and make the most of your time in this vibrant Andalusian capital.

Spain uses the euro (€), and in Seville, cash is still widely used, especially in smaller shops, markets, and traditional tapas bars. While credit and debit cards are generally accepted in hotels, restaurants, and larger stores, it's always a good idea to carry some cash for places that may not accept cards, such as local cafés or family-run businesses. ATMs (*cajeros automáticos*) are easy to find throughout the city, though be mindful of fees if withdrawing from international accounts. To avoid unnecessary charges, opt for ATMs operated by major Spanish banks like Santander, BBVA, or CaixaBank rather than independent ones, which often have higher fees. Tipping in Seville is not obligatory but appreciated—rounding up the bill or leaving a small tip in restaurants, cafés, or for hotel staff is customary but not expected.

Seville is generally a very safe city, but like any popular tourist destination, it's important to stay aware of your surroundings, especially in crowded areas where pickpocketing can occur. The most common spots for petty theft are busy attractions like the Seville Cathedral, Plaza de España, and public transport. Keeping your belongings secure, using a crossbody bag, and avoiding carrying valuables in back pockets will minimize any risk. At night, the city remains lively and safe, particularly in central areas, but if you find yourself in quieter streets alone, exercising standard caution is advisable. Taxis and rideshares are reliable and safe options for late-night travel, and Seville's well-lit streets and friendly atmosphere make walking back from dinner or a flamenco show a pleasant experience.

Respecting local customs will enrich your experience and create positive interactions with the people of Seville. Spaniards, and Andalusians in particular, are known for their warmth and friendliness, and a simple greeting—*hola* (hello) or *buenos días* (good morning)—goes a long way. When entering shops or restaurants, it's customary to greet the staff, and a friendly *gracias* (thank you) upon leaving is always appreciated. The Spanish schedule may take some getting used to, as meals and daily routines run later than in many other countries. Lunch is typically between 2:00 and 4:00 p.m., while dinner often starts around 9:00 p.m. or even later. If you show up to a restaurant at 6:00 p.m. expecting dinner, you may find only drinks and light snacks available.

The concept of a leisurely meal is deeply ingrained in Spanish culture, so don't be surprised if service is relaxed—rushing through a meal is almost unheard of, and lingering over conversation is part of the experience.

When visiting religious sites such as the Seville Cathedral or the Basilica of La Macarena, dressing modestly is a sign of respect. While there is no strict dress code, covering shoulders and avoiding overly short attire is recommended. Photography is generally allowed, but it's always best to check for signs or ask before taking pictures inside churches. In more formal settings, such as high-end restaurants or events, dressing smartly is appreciated, as Sevillanos take pride in their appearance and often dress stylishly.

A final note on local etiquette: Seville has a deep sense of tradition, and festivals like Semana Santa (Holy Week) and Feria de Abril are sacred cultural events. If you visit during these times, watching respectfully and embracing the city's customs—whether it's standing in awe during a solemn religious procession or enjoying the joyous dancing at the fair—will give you a richer, more immersive experience.

By keeping these practical aspects in mind, you'll not only navigate Seville with ease but also gain a deeper appreciation for the city's rhythms, traditions, and way of life, ensuring a visit that is as smooth as it is unforgettable.

CHAPTER 8: SHOPPING AND SOUVENIRS

Handcrafted Ceramics and Flamenco Fashion

Seville is a city of artistry, where tradition and craftsmanship have been passed down for generations, shaping the city's cultural identity. Two of the most iconic expressions of this artistry are handcrafted ceramics and flamenco fashion, both of which tell the story of Seville's deep-rooted heritage through vibrant colors, intricate designs, and meticulous craftsmanship. Whether you're looking for a meaningful souvenir or simply want to admire the dedication of local artisans, exploring these timeless crafts will give you a deeper appreciation of Seville's artistic soul.

Handcrafted ceramics, known as *azulejos*, are an unmistakable part of Seville's aesthetic. You'll see them adorning the facades of buildings, decorating fountains, and lining benches in places like the stunning Plaza de España. These colorful tiles, which date back to the Moorish era, are still made using traditional techniques, with patterns that reflect a blend of Islamic, Renaissance, and Baroque influences. The heart of Seville's ceramics scene is in Triana, the historic pottery district across the river. Here, you can visit workshops where artisans continue the centuries-old practice of hand-painting tiles and pottery, creating everything from decorative plates and vases to intricate wall murals. Shops like *Cerámica Santa Ana* and *Vidal Cerámica* are excellent places to find authentic, high-quality pieces, while the *Centro Cerámica Triana* offers insight into the history of this remarkable craft. If you're looking for a one-of-a-kind keepsake, many workshops allow visitors to customize their own ceramic designs, making for a truly special souvenir.

Just as ceramics are woven into the fabric of Seville's architecture, flamenco fashion is embedded in the city's cultural heartbeat. Nowhere is this more evident than during the Feria de Abril, when locals dress in their finest *trajes de flamenca* (flamenco dresses) and parade through the fairgrounds in a stunning display of color, elegance, and tradition. The flamenco dress, with its fitted silhouette, ruffled sleeves, and vibrant patterns, is an art form in itself—each one carefully designed to enhance movement and exude timeless beauty. While the traditional style remains iconic, modern interpretations have introduced new fabrics, colors, and cuts, keeping flamenco fashion dynamic and ever-evolving.

For those interested in flamenco fashion, the best place to start is in the boutiques and workshops specializing in these exquisite garments. Stores like *Lina 1960*, one of Seville's most renowned flamenco dressmakers, offer beautifully crafted dresses that showcase both tradition and innovation. *Cristina García* and *Pol Núñez* are other designers who have redefined flamenco fashion, incorporating contemporary elements while maintaining the elegance of the classic style. Even if you're not purchasing a dress, accessories such as embroidered shawls (*mantones*), handcrafted combs (*peinetas*), and delicate earrings can be wonderful keepsakes that embody the spirit of flamenco.

Beyond the shops, experiencing flamenco in its true form—on stage—is the best way to appreciate its artistry. Watching a live performance at an *tablao*, such as *Casa de la Memoria* or *El Palacio Andaluz*, will bring to life the dramatic elegance of the dresses as they swirl and flow with the intensity of the dance. The connection between the music, the movement, and the fashion is undeniable, making flamenco not just a performance but a complete sensory experience.

Whether it's the delicate brushstrokes on a ceramic tile or the intricate ruffles of a flamenco dress, these artistic traditions are more than just crafts; they are expressions of Seville's passion, history, and culture. Taking home a piece of Seville—whether a handcrafted ceramic or a beautifully embroidered shawl—means carrying a part of its soul, a reminder of a city where art is not just created but lived.

Best Markets and Shopping Streets

Seville's vibrant markets and shopping streets offer a delightful mix of tradition and modernity, where centuries-old craftsmanship meets contemporary style. Whether you're searching for handcrafted souvenirs, stylish boutiques, or fresh local produce, the city provides an enchanting shopping experience that reflects its rich Andalusian heritage. From bustling food markets to charming pedestrian streets lined with artisanal shops, exploring Seville's retail scene is not just about buying—it's about immersing yourself in the city's culture and lifestyle.

For an authentic taste of local life, the city's markets are a must-visit. The Mercado de Triana, located just across the Isabel II Bridge, is a feast for the senses. Housed in a historic building atop the ruins of the old San Jorge Castle, this market is where locals come for the freshest seafood, Iberian ham, and seasonal produce. Walking through the stalls, you'll find everything from fragrant spices to handmade cheeses, making it the perfect spot to sample Seville's culinary delights or pick up gourmet treats to take home. Beyond food, the market also hosts artisan stands selling ceramics and small handicrafts, making it a wonderful place to browse for unique gifts.

Another fantastic market is the Mercado de la Encarnación, tucked beneath the modern Metropol Parasol. While it may not have the historic charm of Triana's market, it offers an excellent selection of local products and is a great place to experience the city's daily rhythm. After shopping, you can head upstairs to the Parasol's rooftop for breathtaking views of Seville. For those looking for something more alternative, El Jueves Market, held every Thursday on Calle Feria, is the city's oldest open-air flea market. Here, you'll find an eclectic mix of antiques, vintage books, artwork, and second-hand treasures. Whether you're a collector or simply enjoy browsing for unique finds, El Jueves captures the essence of Seville's bohemian spirit.

When it comes to shopping streets, Calle Sierpes is Seville's most famous and one of the best places to start. This pedestrian-friendly thoroughfare, stretching through the heart of the city, is lined with a mix of traditional and contemporary stores. Here, you'll find everything from high-end fashion and jewelry to artisanal leather goods and classic Spanish espadrilles. Nearby, Calle Tetuán and Calle Cuna also offer excellent shopping, with a slightly more upscale feel, featuring stylish boutiques and well-known Spanish brands such as Zara, Mango, and Massimo Dutti.

For those in search of authentic Sevillian craftsmanship, Calle Regina is a hidden gem. This trendy, artsy street is home to small independent shops selling handmade accessories, locally designed clothing, and artisanal goods. One standout store is La Seta Coqueta, which specializes in hand-painted fans, a beautiful and practical souvenir that embodies the elegance of Andalusian culture. Calle Feria, known for its alternative vibe, also has several boutique stores selling handmade jewelry, ceramics, and vintage fashion.

If you're interested in flamenco fashion, Seville's best boutiques can be found around Calle Francos and the Alfalfa district. Here, you'll discover stunning *trajes de flamenca*, embroidered shawls, and handcrafted accessories that showcase the city's passion for flamenco. Whether you're preparing for the Feria de Abril or simply want a piece of flamenco elegance, this area is where to find the most exquisite designs.

Seville's shopping experience is not just about what you buy—it's about the atmosphere, the people, and the centuries of tradition behind every handcrafted item. Whether you're wandering through a lively market, exploring a charming side street, or admiring the work of a skilled artisan, shopping in Seville is an adventure in itself, offering treasures that are as rich and vibrant as the city itself.

Unique Finds to Bring Home

Bringing home a piece of Seville means carrying with you the essence of its history, artistry, and vibrant culture. This city is known for its deep-rooted craftsmanship, where centuries-old traditions continue to thrive in the hands of skilled artisans. Whether you're searching for timeless keepsakes, stylish accessories, or gourmet delights, Seville offers an array of unique finds that go beyond the usual tourist souvenirs. These treasures, infused with the city's soul, will not only remind you of your time in Andalusia but also make for truly special gifts.

Handcrafted ceramics are among the most iconic souvenirs from Seville. The city's signature *azulejos*—colorful, hand-painted tiles—adorn everything from grand palaces to charming neighborhood plazas. In the historic district of Triana, long known as the heart of Seville's ceramics industry, you'll find family-run workshops crafting exquisite plates, bowls, and decorative tiles using techniques passed down for generations. Shops like *Cerámica Santa Ana* and *Vidal Cerámica* offer a stunning selection, with pieces ranging from traditional Moorish patterns to more contemporary styles. If you're looking for something truly personal, some workshops even allow visitors to customize their own ceramic designs, making for a one-of-a-kind keepsake.

For those captivated by the passion of flamenco, bringing home a piece of flamenco fashion is a wonderful way to hold onto the spirit of Seville. The city is home to some of the finest *trajes de flamenca* (flamenco dresses), but even if a full dress isn't practical, beautifully embroidered *mantones de Manila* (silk shawls) or hand-carved *peinetas* (ornamental hair combs) make elegant and wearable souvenirs. Stores like *Lina 1960* and *Cristina García* specialize in high-quality flamenco fashion, offering everything from dramatic ruffled skirts to handcrafted leather dance shoes. Even a delicate pair of flamenco earrings, inspired by the swirling movements of the dance, can bring a touch of Andalusian charm to your wardrobe.

If your tastes lean toward the culinary, Seville's gourmet products make for exquisite gifts and personal indulgences. Spain is famous for its *jamón ibérico*, and bringing home a vacuum-sealed package of this melt-in-your-mouth delicacy ensures you can relive the flavors of Andalusia long after your trip. Local markets such as Mercado de Triana or Mercado de la Encarnación offer high-quality selections, often sourced from nearby Jabugo, the heart of Spain's ham production. Olive oil from Andalusia is another prized find—this region produces some of the finest extra virgin olive oils in the world, with small boutique brands offering organic and artisan varieties. For something sweet, traditional *mantecados* and *polvorones* (crumbly almond cookies) from nearby Estepa make for a delicious taste of southern Spain, while a bottle of *orange wine*, a Seville specialty made from macerated oranges, is a delightful and unique addition to any collection.

Lovers of fragrance will find that Seville, a city famous for its orange blossoms, has inspired exquisite perfumes that capture the scent of Andalusia. Perfumery *Aqua de Sevilla* is well-known for its fresh, citrusy blends, evoking the very essence of springtime in Seville. For something more exclusive, *La Casa del Agua* offers handcrafted perfumes that blend jasmine, neroli, and spices, echoing the aromas of the city's hidden courtyards.

For book lovers and art enthusiasts, beautifully illustrated books on Seville's history, flamenco, or Moorish architecture can be found in boutique bookstores such as *La Extra Vagante* or *Casa Tomada*. Hand-drawn maps, vintage prints of the city's landmarks, and locally crafted leather-bound journals make thoughtful gifts that reflect the city's artistic heritage.

Finally, no visit to Seville would be complete without a traditional *abanico* (Spanish fan). These handcrafted fans, often painted with intricate designs, are both practical and elegant, capturing the timeless style of Sevillian culture. Whether adorned with flamenco motifs, delicate lace, or personalized engravings, a well-made *abanico* is a beautiful keepsake that carries the grace and charm of Andalusia.

Seville's treasures are not just objects—they are pieces of a city that thrives on passion, history, and artistry. Whatever you choose to take home, each item holds a story, a connection to the hands that crafted it, and a reminder of the warmth and magic of Seville, ensuring that your memories of this extraordinary city linger long after your journey ends.

CHAPTER 9: HIDDEN GEMS AND OFF-THE-BEATEN-PATH ADVENTURES

Secret Courtyards and Gardens

Seville is a city that reveals its beauty not all at once, but in layers, like a carefully guarded secret whispered through its ancient streets. Beyond the grand monuments and lively plazas, some of its most enchanting spaces remain hidden behind unassuming facades, waiting to be discovered. The courtyards and gardens of Seville are not just architectural features; they are sanctuaries of tranquility, where time slows down and the city's soul is laid bare in the rustle of palm leaves and the scent of orange blossoms. These secret retreats, often tucked away within palaces, monasteries, and private homes, offer a glimpse into a world of quiet elegance, where Moorish and Andalusian traditions blend in perfect harmony.

The *patio*—the quintessential Sevillian courtyard—is an inheritance from the city's Islamic past, designed to provide shade and coolness in the intense summer heat. Many of these hidden patios still retain their original azulejo-tiled walls, carved wooden balconies, and central fountains, creating an oasis of serenity amid the vibrant energy of the city. One of the most breathtaking examples is found within the Casa de Pilatos, a lesser-known palace that rivals the grandeur of the Alcázar. Step through its gates, and you are transported into a dream of Renaissance elegance fused with Mudejar artistry, where cascading bougainvillea and delicate stucco carvings frame a courtyard of perfect symmetry.

For a more intimate glimpse into Sevillian life, the *Palacio de las Dueñas* offers another hidden jewel. This aristocratic mansion, once home to the Duchess of Alba, conceals an exquisite series of courtyards filled with orange trees, trickling fountains, and climbing roses. The scent of jasmine lingers in the air, blending with the distant echoes of the city, creating an atmosphere that feels both timeless and deeply personal.

Beyond palatial estates, some of Seville's most secret courtyards lie behind the thick walls of its ancient monasteries and convents. The *Convento de Santa Paula*, a working convent dating back to the 15th century, opens its doors to those who seek a moment of quiet reflection. Its cloistered courtyard, shaded by olive trees and lined with intricate ceramic tiles, offers a glimpse into a world of devotion and contemplation, untouched by time. The nuns here sell handmade sweets—delicate *yemas de San Leandro* and almond pastries—adding to the sense of stepping into a tradition preserved for centuries.

Equally mesmerizing are the gardens that lie hidden behind the city's grand buildings, offering a respite from the sun-drenched streets. The *Jardines del Real Alcázar* are the most famous, but few visitors take the time to truly wander through their many levels, discovering shaded pavilions, whispering fountains, and pathways lined with fragrant myrtle. If you stray beyond the more frequented areas, you'll find secluded spots where the only sound is the cooing of doves and the gentle murmur of water—a sensory retreat that feels worlds away from the bustling crowds.

But some of the most magical spaces are those that are not in guidebooks at all, the patios of private homes that reveal themselves only once a year during the *Festival de los Patios*. Held in May, this tradition allows visitors a rare glimpse into the most beautiful and meticulously tended courtyards of Seville, where residents proudly open their doors to showcase the lush greenery, hanging geraniums, and centuries-old wells that make their homes so enchanting. Walking through the labyrinthine streets of the Santa Cruz or San Bartolomé districts, you might catch a glimpse of one of these hidden sanctuaries through an open gate—just a momentary view of a world that remains mostly unseen.

Seville's secret courtyards and gardens remind us that the true heart of the city is not always found in its grand avenues or famous landmarks, but in the quiet, intimate spaces where history, nature, and artistry intertwine. They are places to linger, to breathe, to lose yourself in the play of light and shadow on a tiled wall, to listen to the stories whispered in the rustling leaves. To discover them is to truly know Seville—not just as a visitor, but as someone who has been invited into its hidden soul.

Lesser-Known Museums and Local Hangouts

Seville is a city of grand spectacles, where the Alcázar dazzles with its intricate Mudejar artistry and the Giralda towers above a skyline of terracotta rooftops. But beyond the iconic landmarks, there's another Seville—one that lives in its tucked-away museums, intimate cultural spaces, and local hangouts where the city's pulse beats strongest. It's in these lesser-known corners that Seville reveals itself most authentically, offering a deeper connection to its history, art, and everyday rhythm.

Among the city's hidden cultural gems, the *Museo del Baile Flamenco* stands out as an intimate tribute to Seville's most passionate art form. Nestled in the winding streets of the Santa Cruz district, this museum—founded by the legendary dancer Cristina Hoyos—goes beyond mere exhibition. Here, flamenco is not just something to be observed but felt, with immersive audiovisual displays, costumes worn by some of the greatest performers, and live shows that bring the space to life each evening. For those who want to delve even deeper, dance workshops allow visitors to experience the raw intensity of flamenco firsthand, making this much more than just a museum—it's a gateway into Seville's soul.

For a glimpse into Seville's eclectic artistic side, the *Centro Andaluz de Arte Contemporáneo* (CAAC) offers a striking contrast to the city's historic opulence. Housed in a former monastery turned ceramics factory, this avant-garde space showcases contemporary Spanish and international art, with exhibits ranging from experimental photography to thought-provoking installations. But the museum is as much about atmosphere as it is about art—its gardens, courtyards, and even the remnants of the old kiln give it a unique, almost meditative quality. Unlike the more crowded museums of the city center, CAAC invites you to linger, to sit beneath the orange trees, and to let modern creativity meet centuries of history in a space that feels both raw and poetic.

History lovers will find another hidden treasure in the *Archivo General de Indias*, a quiet sanctuary that holds some of the most important documents from Spain's Age of Exploration. While many visitors rush past it on their way to the Cathedral, those who step inside discover a world of yellowed maps, royal decrees, and handwritten letters that chart the course of Spain's colonial empire. Walking through its grand halls, with their towering wooden shelves and faint scent of old parchment, one can almost hear the whispers of conquistadors and navigators whose stories shaped the world.

But museums are only part of Seville's hidden charm—its true magic lies in its everyday spaces, the local hangouts where Sevillanos gather to eat, drink, and enjoy life. One such place is *La Carbonería*, a bohemian bar tucked away in a nondescript building in the old Jewish quarter. There are no neon signs or flashy advertisements, just an open-air patio, wooden benches, and an atmosphere of unpretentious authenticity. It's one of the best places in the city to catch spontaneous flamenco performances, where guitarists, singers, and dancers pour their hearts into the music, not for tourists but for the love of the art itself.

For a more modern take on Seville's nightlife, *Sala X* is a hidden gem that hosts an eclectic mix of live music, from indie rock to experimental jazz. Housed in a former cinema, this venue has become a favorite among locals looking for an alternative to the city's traditional taverns. And then there's *Calle Pérez Galdós*, an unassuming street that has quietly become a hotspot for cocktail bars and small, stylish eateries. Places like *Perro Chiko* and *The Second Room* offer expertly crafted drinks and a laid-back, creative vibe, making this area a favorite among Seville's young artists and musicians.

For those who prefer a daytime retreat, the *Jardines de Murillo* provide an unexpected escape from the tourist-filled streets. While many visitors head straight to the nearby Alcázar, these gardens—shaded by towering ficus trees and lined with ceramic benches—offer a moment of quiet reflection. Locals come here to read, sketch, or simply enjoy the golden afternoon light filtering through the leaves. It's the kind of place where time slows down, where you can sit with a coffee and watch the world go by, feeling like you've stumbled upon a secret part of Seville that few take the time to notice.

Seville's hidden museums and local hangouts remind us that the true spirit of the city isn't found only in its grand cathedrals or famous plazas. It lives in the dimly lit bars where flamenco is played with wild abandon, in the quiet halls where ancient manuscripts whisper forgotten stories, in the gardens where locals stop to rest under the shade of an orange tree. To truly know Seville, one must step off the well-trodden path, slow down, and let the city reveal itself, one secret at a time.

Quirky Spots That Will Surprise You

Seville is a city that thrives on the unexpected. Beyond its grand palaces, historic cathedrals, and lively tapas bars, there are places that defy expectations—hidden corners, offbeat attractions, and surreal spots that make you pause, smile, and realize just how much more there is to discover. Whether it's a mysterious chapel covered in skulls, a secret rooftop with a view unlike any other, or a centuries-old tradition that feels straight out of a fairy tale, these quirky spots will surprise even the most seasoned traveler.

Tucked away in a quiet corner of the Macarena district is one of Seville's strangest and most fascinating sites: the *Chapel of San José de la Montaña*. While from the outside it looks like a humble church, step inside and you'll find a macabre yet mesmerizing altar adorned with real human skulls. These are not meant to frighten but to remind visitors of the fleeting nature of life, a theme deeply rooted in Spanish religious tradition. It's eerie, it's beautiful, and it's one of the city's most unexpected hidden gems.

For something completely different, the *Antiquarium de las Setas* takes you underground—literally. Beneath the futuristic wooden structure of Metropol Parasol, a glass-floored museum showcases the well-preserved ruins of a Roman city that once thrived here. It's a fascinating clash of the ancient and the ultra-modern, where you can walk over mosaics and ancient fish-salting vats while knowing that just above you, people are sipping cocktails on one of Seville's most cutting-edge rooftops. The contrast is surreal, but that's exactly what makes this place so unforgettable.

Speaking of rooftops, Seville has no shortage of panoramic viewpoints, but few are as quirky as *La Terraza del EME*, a bar perched atop a hotel that offers breathtaking views of the Cathedral. What makes it unique isn't just the perspective, but the stylish, almost cinematic atmosphere. It feels like the kind of place where James Bond might meet a mysterious informant—if Bond had a taste for Seville's finest *tinto de verano*.

Then there's *La Casa de la Ciencia*, a museum housed in a grand neoclassical building that once belonged to the 1929 Ibero-American Exposition. What makes it quirky? It's not just any science museum—it's a science museum inside a former palace, featuring everything from giant fossils to deep-sea creatures, plus a small but fascinating planetarium. It's an odd yet charming mix of aristocratic elegance and hands-on science, making it a great place for curious minds of all ages.

If you're in the mood for something truly surreal, head to *Callejón del Agua*, a tiny alleyway that runs along the walls of the Alcázar. At first glance, it seems like just another picturesque Sevillian street, but it holds a fascinating secret: legend has it that the walls once carried water from the palace gardens, creating a cooling system that kept the noble houses along the alley refreshingly cool in summer. Whether or not the legend is entirely true, there's something undeniably magical about wandering this narrow, shaded path, hearing nothing but the occasional drip of a fountain nearby.

And then there's *El Palacio de la Condesa de Lebrija*, a lesser-known mansion in the heart of the city that feels like something out of an Indiana Jones movie. The Countess of Lebrija, an eccentric aristocrat, had a passion for archaeology and spent her life collecting ancient artifacts, mosaics, and sculptures. The result? A house-museum where you can walk across perfectly preserved Roman mosaics while admiring Greek urns, Islamic tiles, and even Egyptian relics. It's a collector's paradise, a historian's dream, and an utterly unexpected treasure trove in the middle of Seville.

For those who love bizarre traditions, the *Tunas Universitarias* are an absolute must-see. No, this isn't about fish—*tunas* are groups of university students who dress in medieval-style outfits, play traditional Spanish music, and serenade passersby in the streets of Seville. This centuries-old tradition is equal parts charming, theatrical, and slightly absurd, but it's a delightful reminder of how much history and fun coexist in this city. If you're lucky, you might stumble upon a *tuna* group performing in Plaza Nueva or near the Cathedral, their lively songs filling the night air with an energy that is impossible to resist.

Seville's quirky spots remind us that this city is not just about grand monuments and historic tales—it's about the unexpected, the playful, and the utterly unique. It's a place where past and present, tradition and eccentricity, coexist in the most delightful ways. The best way to discover these surprises? Wander, explore, and let Seville reveal its secrets one curious corner at a time.

CHAPTER 10: SEVILLE BY SEASON

Spring: The City in Full Bloom

Spring in Seville is not just a season; it is a transformation. The city emerges from winter's mild slumber with a burst of color, scent, and celebration, draping itself in the fragrance of orange blossoms and the rhythms of flamenco. This is the time when Seville is at its most poetic, a place where every square, courtyard, and riverside promenade feels touched by something magical. The soft warmth of the Andalusian sun bathes the city in golden light, while locals and visitors alike take to the streets to revel in the beauty of a city that seems to have been designed for this very moment.

The season begins with a quiet enchantment—the orange trees, which have stood like silent sentinels all winter, suddenly explode into bloom. The scent of *azahar* drifts through the city, carried on the breeze down cobblestone alleys and past the grand facades of palaces and churches. It is a fragrance unlike any other—sweet, citrusy, and nostalgic, as if the very soul of Seville has been distilled into the air. Walking through Santa Cruz or along the Paseo de las Delicias in early spring, one cannot help but pause and breathe it in, letting the city's essence settle into memory.

But spring in Seville is not only about quiet beauty—it is also about grandeur, tradition, and spectacle. Semana Santa, the Holy Week leading up to Easter, transforms the city into a living work of art. By day, the streets are filled with solemn processions, where immense, gold-laden floats carrying statues of Christ and the Virgin Mary glide through the crowds, carried on the shoulders of devoted *costaleros*. By night, flickering candlelight illuminates the faces of penitents in their traditional robes, and the haunting strains of a lone *saeta* sung from a balcony can send chills down the spine. It is a week of contrasts—sorrow and devotion balanced with an indescribable beauty that captivates even those who do not share in its religious significance.

And then, just as the somber echoes of Semana Santa fade, the city erupts into its most joyous celebration: the Feria de Abril. Seville's fairground, *El Real de la Feria*, becomes a temporary city of its own, where striped tents—*casetas*— line the avenues, filled with laughter, music, and the swirling skirts of flamenco dresses. Horse-drawn carriages parade past as locals dressed in elegant *trajes de corto* and vibrant *trajes de gitana* sip glasses of chilled *rebujito* and dance *sevillanas* with an effortless grace that can only be learned from childhood. The fair is a world apart, a place where time seems to stand still and where Seville's passion for life is on full display. To visit during Feria is to see the city at its most exuberant, where the nights stretch long into dawn and every corner of the fairground pulses with energy.

Yet, beyond the grand events, spring is also the season to simply wander and take in the city at its best. The gardens of the Alcázar become a paradise of wisteria and roses, their fountains murmuring softly under the warmth of the sun. The banks of the Guadalquivir invite lazy afternoon strolls, where the reflection of the Torre del Oro shimmers on the water like a mirage. Café terraces spill onto the streets, offering the perfect spot to sip coffee or a cool glass of *tinto de verano*, watching as the world passes by in slow, sun-drenched motion.

Spring in Seville is an invitation—to celebrate, to explore, to savor. It is the season when the city sheds any restraint and offers itself fully, with all its scents, sounds, and sensations. It is a time of poetry, of music, of light and warmth. To experience Seville in the spring is to understand why so many have fallen in love with it, why it lingers in the heart long after the season has passed.

Summer: How to Stay Cool and Still Enjoy It

Summer in Seville is not for the faint of heart. The city basks in the full force of the Andalusian sun, its golden light turning the rooftops into a shimmering mirage. With daytime temperatures often soaring past 40°C (104°F), the streets slow down, and the city moves to a different rhythm—one of adaptation, patience, and knowing where to find shade and cool relief. But while summer in Seville can be intense, it is far from unbearable. In fact, with the right approach, it offers a uniquely enchanting experience, one where the city reveals a quieter, more intimate side that many visitors never see.

The key to enjoying Seville in summer is to follow the wisdom of the locals. The day begins early, before the sun climbs too high, with a morning stroll through the shaded alleys of Barrio Santa Cruz or along the Guadalquivir River, where the air still carries a hint of coolness from the night before. The gardens of the Alcázar are particularly magical at this hour, their fountains murmuring softly as the first rays of sunlight filter through the palm trees. This is the time for exploration, for slipping into the cool embrace of the city's churches, where thick stone walls provide a sanctuary from the growing heat outside.

By midday, the sun reigns supreme, and Seville surrenders to its command. The streets empty, shops close, and the city retreats indoors for the sacred ritual of *siesta*. This is not just a nap—it is a way of life, a necessary pause in the day that allows Sevillanos to endure the heat with grace. For visitors, this is the perfect time to embrace the slow pace of summer, finding refuge in an air-conditioned museum, a shaded café, or even a traditional bathhouse like *Aire de Sevilla*, where cool stone pools offer a welcome respite.

Even the food adjusts to the season. Heavy meals are abandoned in favor of light, refreshing dishes. A bowl of *gazpacho* or *salmorejo*, chilled and bursting with the flavors of ripe tomatoes and olive oil, becomes not just a dish but a necessity. Plates of *jamón ibérico*, served with slices of juicy melon, offer the perfect salty-sweet contrast. And then there's *tinto de verano*, the drink of choice in summer—a simple yet perfect mix of red wine and sparkling lemon soda, served over ice, designed to refresh and revive.

As the afternoon stretches on, the city begins to stir once more. By early evening, the sun's grip loosens, and Seville slowly comes back to life. This is the golden hour, when the streets fill with the sound of conversation, and the terraces of Triana and Alameda de Hércules become the city's living rooms. Rooftop bars, like *Terraza Atalaya* or *La Terraza del EME*, offer breathtaking views of the Cathedral as the sky melts into shades of pink and orange.

And then, when the heat finally fades into the warm embrace of night, Seville becomes truly magical. Flamenco sounds even more passionate in the stillness of the evening, the rhythmic claps and mournful voices echoing through hidden courtyards. The city's plazas, quiet and sun-drenched by day, now hum with life, filled with couples strolling hand in hand, families enjoying ice cream, and musicians playing softly in the corners. Late dinners stretch long into the night, as plates of grilled seafood and cold *cerveza* keep the conversation flowing.

To visit Seville in summer is to surrender to a different kind of time, one dictated by the rise and fall of the sun. It is to seek out shade and cool tiles, to embrace the night as the real heart of the city, and to understand that slowness is not laziness but survival. The heat may be formidable, but so is Seville's beauty—and if you let the city guide you, you'll find that even in the height of summer, it remains irresistible.

Autumn and Winter: A Different Kind of Magic

Autumn and winter in Seville bring a transformation that feels almost like a well-kept secret. While spring and summer steal the spotlight with their grand festivities and golden sunlight, the cooler months reveal a different kind of magic—one of crisp, golden afternoons, quiet streets, and a city that seems to breathe a little deeper. The crowds thin, the pace slows, and Seville becomes a place of subtle beauty, where the scent of roasted chestnuts drifts through the air and the soft glow of lanterns reflects off rain-kissed cobblestones.

Autumn arrives gently, easing Seville out of the intense summer heat and into a season of warm afternoons and pleasantly cool evenings. By late September, the city sheds its slower summer rhythm and begins to pulse with renewed energy. The parks, especially María Luisa and the gardens of the Alcázar, turn into a painter's palette of deep reds and golds. The Guadalquivir River, bathed in the softer autumn light, becomes the perfect place for a leisurely boat ride or a sunset stroll along its banks.

This is also the time when Seville's cultural season flourishes. The Teatro de la Maestranza fills with the sounds of opera and classical music, while flamenco clubs, or *tablaos*, begin hosting some of their most intense performances of the year. Flamenco, raw and deeply emotional, seems even more haunting against the backdrop of autumn's cool nights. Festivals continue, too—early November brings *Día de los Difuntos* (All Souls' Day), when the city's churches are filled with candlelight, and locals visit cemeteries to honor their loved ones. There's a quiet reverence in the air, a contrast to the exuberance of Seville's spring festivals but just as moving.

By December, Seville embraces winter, though here, winter is never harsh. Instead of snow, there are crisp mornings and gentle rains that make the orange trees glow even brighter. The city dresses up for Christmas, with fairy lights strung across the avenues and nativity scenes—*belénes*—set up in churches and shop windows. The Christmas markets open, offering everything from handmade ceramics to marzipan sweets shaped like tiny fruits. One of the most enchanting sights of the season is the illumination of Avenida de la Constitución, where the Giralda stands tall against the backdrop of twinkling lights.

Winter in Seville is a time for cozy traditions. Churros and thick, velvety *chocolate caliente* become the perfect morning indulgence, best enjoyed in a small café as the city slowly wakes. The scent of cinnamon and anise drifts from bakeries preparing *tortas de aceite*, crisp and flaky pastries that have been a local favorite for centuries. And for those seeking warmth, a glass of *vino de naranja*, Seville's famous orange-infused wine, offers a taste of the city's citrus-filled heart.

The New Year arrives with a uniquely Spanish tradition—eating twelve grapes at midnight, one for each chime of the clock, to bring good luck for the year ahead. Plaza Nueva and other main squares fill with people celebrating under the stars, while bars and restaurants keep their doors open late for those who want to welcome the year with a final toast.

And then, just when the holiday season seems to be ending, Seville saves one of its most beloved traditions for last: *Los Reyes Magos* (Three Kings' Day) on January 6th. More important than Christmas for many Spaniards, this is when children receive their gifts, and the city comes alive with parades featuring the Three Wise Men, who toss candy into the crowds. Families gather for one final feast, sharing slices of *Roscón de Reyes*, a sweet, ring-shaped cake hiding a tiny figurine inside—a surprise that will determine who gets to wear the paper crown for the day.

Autumn and winter in Seville are not about spectacle but about atmosphere. They offer a chance to see the city in a quieter, more intimate way—to linger in a café without rush, to explore the winding streets without the heat, to appreciate the simple beauty of a city that never loses its charm, no matter the season. Whether it's the golden light of an autumn afternoon or the glow of lanterns on a winter's evening, Seville in these months is nothing short of enchanting.

CHAPTER 11: ITINERARY PLAN

3-Days itinerary

Here's a seamless three-day itinerary that allows you to experience Seville's rich history, vibrant culture, and undeniable charm while keeping a natural flow to your exploration. The city is best enjoyed at a leisurely pace, taking in the details—the scent of orange blossoms, the echo of flamenco in a quiet alley, the warmth of the sun on a terrace with a glass of wine. This itinerary is designed to give you a deep and immersive experience without rushing from one landmark to the next.

Day One: The Historic Heart of Seville

Begin your journey in the heart of Seville's old town, where history, grandeur, and Moorish influences weave together in the city's most iconic landmarks. Start at the **Seville Cathedral**, one of the largest Gothic cathedrals in the world, and take your time admiring its intricate chapels, the tomb of Christopher Columbus, and the breathtaking main altar. Climb **La Giralda**, the former minaret turned bell tower, for sweeping views of the city bathed in the morning light.

From here, step into the ethereal world of the **Alcázar of Seville**, a palace that feels like something out of a dream, with its intricate Moorish arches, dazzling tilework, and lush gardens filled with fountains and palm trees. Take your time exploring its halls and courtyards, where every detail tells a story of sultans and kings.

As you emerge from the Alcázar, wander into **Barrio Santa Cruz**, the city's former Jewish Quarter, where narrow alleyways twist and turn in a maze of whitewashed houses, hidden courtyards, and bougainvillea-covered balconies. Find a quiet café to stop for a traditional **salmorejo**, a cold tomato soup that is as refreshing as it is delicious.

Spend the afternoon meandering through the **Archivo de Indias**, where Spain's colonial history is preserved in thousands of ancient documents. As the sun begins to dip, stroll to the **Metropol Parasol**, the city's striking modern landmark, and head to its rooftop for panoramic sunset views over the rooftops of Seville. End the day with a relaxed dinner in the Alameda de Hércules district, where trendy bars and local eateries serve everything from classic **jamón ibérico** to innovative tapas.

Day Two: The Riverside and the Soul of Flamenco

Start the morning with a walk along the **Guadalquivir River**, where you'll find a different side of Seville—one where the breeze carries the scent of the water, and rowers glide past historic bridges. Visit the **Torre del Oro**, the golden-hued watchtower that once guarded the city, and step inside to learn about Seville's naval history.

Cross the **Puente de Isabel II** into **Triana**, the city's most vibrant and authentic neighborhood, known for its flamenco heritage and ceramic workshops. Wander through **Calle Betis**, where colorful houses line the river, and pop into one of the many artisan shops selling beautifully hand-painted ceramics. For lunch, find a cozy **bodega** and try **pescaito frito**, a plate of lightly fried fish served with a squeeze of lemon.

In the afternoon, take a detour to **Plaza de España**, one of the most breathtaking spots in Seville. Its semi-circular structure, adorned with elaborate tilework representing Spain's provinces, is a masterpiece of architectural grandeur. Take a slow walk around the plaza or rent a rowboat to paddle through the small canal that encircles it.

As night falls, it's time to experience the **soul of Seville— flamenco**. Head to an intimate **tablao** like Casa de la Memoria or Los Gallos, where passionate dancers, singers, and guitarists bring the art form to life with raw emotion. Flamenco is not just a performance; it's an experience, one that stays with you long after the final notes fade.

Day Three: Hidden Gems and a Taste of Andalusia

After two days of intense sightseeing, the third day is about slowing down and discovering the city's lesser-known treasures. Start your morning in the **Palacio de las Dueñas**, a stunning mansion filled with Andalusian charm, lavish gardens, and a fascinating history tied to the noble House of Alba.

Then, make your way to the **Mercado de Triana**, where the morning buzz of locals picking up fresh produce, seafood, and spices fills the air. Grab a snack or a fresh juice, and soak in the lively atmosphere of this market built atop the remains of an ancient castle.

Spend the afternoon escaping into the tranquility of the **Casa de Pilatos**, a hidden gem that blends Mudejar, Gothic, and Renaissance styles in a dazzling display of architecture. The palace's courtyards, fountains, and beautifully tiled rooms make it one of the most underrated yet breathtaking spots in Seville.

For a final indulgence, take part in a **tapas and wine tour**, hopping between local taverns and bodegas where traditional Andalusian flavors come to life. Try **solomillo al whisky** (pork loin in whiskey sauce), **espinacas con garbanzos** (spinach with chickpeas), and finish with a glass of **vino de naranja**, Seville's famous orange-infused wine.

As the night settles, take one last slow walk along the river, watching the city lights shimmer on the water, and let Seville leave its final imprint on you—a city of history, passion, and timeless beauty, where every corner holds a story waiting to be discovered.

1-week Itinerary

A full week in Seville allows you to experience the city in a way that goes beyond the usual must-sees. You won't just visit the grand monuments—you'll sink into the rhythm of life here, lingering in sun-dappled plazas, savoring long lunches, and discovering hidden corners that most travelers miss. This seven-day itinerary balances history, culture, food, day trips, and the pure joy of simply being in Seville, letting the city unfold at a natural, unhurried pace.

Day One: The Historic Heart and an Introduction to Seville

Arriving in Seville, you'll want to start in its most iconic and breathtaking spots. Begin at the **Seville Cathedral**, an architectural marvel that dominates the skyline. Inside, lose yourself in its vast halls, admire the tomb of Christopher Columbus, and then climb **La Giralda**, the towering former minaret, for a panoramic view that reveals the city's rooftops and beyond.

From here, step into the mesmerizing **Alcázar of Seville**, a palace where centuries of history are carved into intricate Moorish archways, ceramic tiles, and lush gardens that whisper stories of kings and sultans. Wander through the courtyards, stopping to admire the interplay of light and water in the fountains.

After emerging from the Alcázar, the winding alleys of **Barrio Santa Cruz** await. This old Jewish Quarter, with its secret courtyards, flower-filled balconies, and labyrinthine streets, feels like stepping into another era. Take your time, find a quiet **taberna**, and indulge in your first taste of **salmorejo** or **espinacas con garbanzos**.

As the evening settles, head to **Metropol Parasol**, an undulating wooden structure that offers an unbeatable sunset view over the city. Let the soft, golden light mark the end of your first day before heading to a relaxed dinner in the Alameda de Hércules area, where both traditional and modern tapas bars flourish.

Day Two: Plaza de España, Triana, and Flamenco's Heartbeat

Start your day in **Plaza de España**, one of the most breathtaking public squares in Spain. Stroll beneath its grand arches, admire the tiled alcoves representing Spain's provinces, and perhaps even take a small boat ride along the canal. Next, wander into **María Luisa Park**, a vast, shaded retreat filled with fountains, exotic plants, and hidden corners perfect for a peaceful pause.

Cross the **Puente de Isabel II** into **Triana**, a neighborhood that pulses with authenticity. This is the cradle of flamenco, where artisans still hand-paint ceramics in small workshops and where tapas bars are packed with locals enjoying **pescaito frito** and **manzanilla sherry**. Spend time exploring, pop into the **Mercado de Triana**, and watch life unfold along **Calle Betis**, which runs parallel to the river.

As night falls, it's time for a true **flamenco experience**. Book a show at an intimate **tablao**, where the raw, passionate performance will stay with you long after the final notes fade.

Day Three: Hidden Palaces, Local Markets, and Rooftop Views

Seville isn't just about grand monuments; it's also about discovering its quieter, more intimate corners. Begin at the **Palacio de las Dueñas**, a stunning noble residence with exquisite gardens, intricate tiles, and a rich history tied to Spanish aristocracy.

Then, dive into Seville's food culture at the **Mercado de Triana** or **Mercado de la Encarnación**, where fresh produce, Iberian ham, and local cheeses create an irresistible sensory experience.

Spend the afternoon meandering through the **Casa de Pilatos**, a hidden gem blending Mudejar, Gothic, and Renaissance styles in an architectural symphony. Then, treat yourself to a drink at one of Seville's **rooftop bars**, such as La Terraza del EME, where the views of the illuminated Giralda are nothing short of magical.

Day Four: A Day Trip to Córdoba and the Mesmerizing Mezquita

While Seville is intoxicating, a journey to **Córdoba** offers a different kind of wonder. Just a short train ride away, Córdoba is home to the **Mezquita**, a former mosque turned cathedral that is one of Spain's most breathtaking sights. Walk beneath its forest of red-and-white arches, a masterpiece of Islamic architecture, before stepping into the serene courtyards of the **Alcázar de los Reyes Cristianos**.

Stroll through **Córdoba's Jewish Quarter**, where whitewashed houses and flower-filled patios create a postcard-perfect scene. Enjoy a leisurely lunch in a shaded plaza before returning to Seville in the evening, where a relaxed dinner at a traditional **bodega** awaits.

Day Five: Doñana National Park or Jerez de la Frontera

Today is about stepping outside Seville once more, either to experience **Andalusia's wild side** or its world-famous **sherry culture**.

- **Option 1: Doñana National Park**: If nature calls, head to **Doñana**, a vast expanse of wetlands, dunes, and forests where flamingos, Iberian lynxes, and wild horses roam. A guided tour takes you through the park's ever-changing landscapes, offering a glimpse into Spain's most important ecological reserve.
- **Option 2: Jerez de la Frontera**: If you prefer a day of wine and tradition, Jerez is the birthplace of **sherry wine** and the home of **Andalusian equestrian art**. Visit a historic bodega, learn about the sherry-making process, and sip your way through its different varieties. If you time your visit right, you can also watch an **equestrian ballet** at the Royal Andalusian School of Equestrian Art.

Return to Seville for an easy-going evening, perhaps wandering the atmospheric streets of the **Macarena district**.

Day Six: Lesser-Known Museums, Secret Courtyards, and a Slow Day in Seville

After so much exploration, today is about **slow travel**. Visit a lesser-known museum like the **Hospital de los Venerables**, a beautiful 17th-century baroque building now home to a remarkable art collection. Then, seek out the city's **hidden courtyards**, like those tucked away in Barrio San Bartolomé, where time seems to stand still.

Linger in **Plaza del Salvador**, where Sevillanos gather for a midday beer, and soak in the relaxed energy of the city. The afternoon is perfect for one last deep dive into Seville's **ceramic culture**, picking up a handcrafted souvenir before a **final sunset along the river**.

Day Seven: A Leisurely Farewell to Seville

On your final morning, take a last, unhurried walk through the city, perhaps enjoying a final cup of **chocolate con churros** in a historic café. If time allows, visit the **Basilica de la Macarena**, home to Seville's most beloved Virgin, before wandering through the quiet streets one last time.

Seville leaves an imprint on those who visit—not just through its grand monuments, but in the rhythm of its life, the warmth of its people, and the way every moment seems touched by beauty. As you depart, you carry a piece of Seville with you, a memory of golden light, music, and the soul of Andalusia.

CONCLUSION

How to Make the Most of Your Trip

Making the most of your trip to Seville is about more than just ticking off famous landmarks—it's about immersing yourself in the city's rhythm, embracing its unhurried pace, and savoring every detail that makes it one of Spain's most captivating destinations. Whether it's through lingering over a long meal, getting lost in its hidden alleyways, or listening to the echoes of flamenco in the night, Seville is a city best enjoyed with all the senses.

Start by letting go of rigid schedules. Seville is a place that rewards spontaneity—turning down an unplanned street might lead to a sunlit square where locals gather over coffee, or a tiny courtyard bursting with jasmine and orange blossoms. The joy is in wandering, in discovering a small family-run **bodega** that serves the best **jamón ibérico** you've ever tasted, or in stumbling upon a flamenco rehearsal in an unassuming corner of **Triana**.

Time your visits wisely. The golden hours of early morning and late evening are when Seville is at its most magical. If you visit in the warmer months, embrace the **Spanish siesta culture**—sightseeing in the peak afternoon heat is exhausting, so follow the local rhythm: explore in the morning, rest in the afternoon, and come alive again in the evening when the city is bathed in soft, golden light.

Embrace **tapas culture**, but do it the right way. Rather than sitting down for a large meal, hop from one tapas bar to another, trying a different specialty at each place. A glass of

fino sherry with **pescaito frito** at one spot, a plate of **solomillo al whisky** at another—this is how Sevillanos dine, and it's the best way to experience the city's culinary richness.

Go beyond the main attractions. While the **Alcázar, the Cathedral, and Plaza de España** are breathtaking, some of Seville's greatest treasures are in its quieter corners. Seek out the **Casa de Pilatos**, a stunning yet less-crowded palace. Visit **Hospital de los Venerables**, a beautifully preserved Baroque building in the heart of Santa Cruz. Explore the **Palacio de las Dueñas**, a noble residence filled with Andalusian charm.

If you truly want to understand Seville, you must experience **flamenco**. Not just by watching a polished show at a tablao, but by feeling its raw energy in a **peña**, where locals gather for spontaneous, heartfelt performances. The best flamenco is not always advertised—it happens in the depths of the night, in small bars, in whispered recommendations from those who know.

Slow down and observe the details. Notice the patterns of the **azulejos** (ceramic tiles) that cover the buildings, the scent of orange trees that perfumes the air, the way locals greet each other with warmth and familiarity. The essence of Seville isn't just in its grand sights—it's in these everyday moments, in the way life unfolds effortlessly in its sun-drenched streets.

Finally, leave room for serendipity. Plan, but not too much. Some of the best memories in Seville come from moments you never expected—an impromptu street performance in Alameda de Hércules, a quiet afternoon spent people-watching in Plaza del Salvador, a conversation with a local who shares a hidden gem you wouldn't have found otherwise. The real magic of Seville isn't just in seeing it, but in **feeling it**, in letting it reveal itself to you at its own pace.

Seville's Timeless Allure

Seville's timeless allure lies not only in its grand monuments and storied past but in the way the city makes you feel— wrapped in warmth, color, and the rhythm of a place that knows how to savor life. It is a city that refuses to rush, where long afternoons stretch into golden evenings, where laughter spills from lively plazas, and where history and modern life intertwine effortlessly. Seville doesn't just invite you to explore; it seduces you into staying longer than you planned, lingering a little more in its sunlit courtyards, and losing yourself in the poetry of its streets.

There is a reason why Seville has inspired artists, poets, and travelers for centuries. Its architecture tells stories of conquest and coexistence, where Moorish palaces stand beside Gothic cathedrals, and Renaissance façades blend seamlessly with Baroque splendor. The **Alcázar**, with its delicate arches and whispering fountains, transports you to the days of sultans and kings. The **Giralda**, once a minaret and now the city's iconic bell tower, offers a glimpse into Seville's layered history. The **Plaza de España**, a masterpiece of ceramic tilework and sweeping grandeur, is both a monument and an invitation to dream.

But beyond its history, Seville's magic is found in its everyday moments. It's in the scent of orange blossoms that fills the air in spring, in the sound of a lone flamenco guitarist strumming in a quiet square, in the way the light dances off the Guadalquivir River at sunset. It's in the tradition of an afternoon **tapeo**, hopping from one bar to another, tasting the essence of Andalusian cuisine in small, flavorful bites. It's in the deep, haunting wail of **cante jondo**, the purest form of flamenco, that reaches into the soul and leaves you breathless.

To visit Seville is to step into a world that feels both timeless and alive, where past and present embrace in a dance as passionate as the city itself. Whether it's your first time here or your tenth, Seville always finds a way to surprise you, to capture a piece of your heart, and to remind you that some places are meant to be experienced slowly, with all the senses engaged. This is not just a city—it's a feeling, a melody, a moment suspended in time. And once you've felt its pull, you will always long to return.

Printed in Dunstable, United Kingdom

76733178R00067